Shattered Stones,
Scattered Seeds

Shattered Stones, Scattered Seeds

The Story of a Shtetl
and a Family
Who Lived There

Myrna Neuringer Levy

IGUANA

Publisher: Greg Ioannou
Editor: Ruth Chernia
Front cover image: courtesy of the Neuringer family
Front cover design: Meghan Behse
Book layout: Kate Unrau

Library and Archives Canada Cataloguing in Publication

Levy, Myrna Neuringer, author
    Shattered stones, scattered seeds : the story of a shtetl and a family who lived there / Myrna Neuringer Levy.

Includes bibliographical references.
Issued in print and electronic formats.
ISBN 978-1-77180-096-9 (pbk.).--ISBN 978-1-77180-097-6 (epub).--ISBN 978-1-77180-098-3 (kindle)

    1. Levy, Myrna Neuringer--Family. 2. Neuringer, Leib Yosef, born 1843--Family. 3. Neuringer family. 4. Jews--Ukraine--Borshchiv (Ternopilʹsʹka oblastʹ)--Biography. 5. Shtetls--Ukraine--Borshchiv (Ternopilʹsʹka oblastʹ)--History. 6. Borshchiv (Ternopilʹsʹka oblastʹ, Ukraine)--Biography. 7. Holocaust, Jewish (1939-1945)--Ukraine--orshchiv (Ternopilʹsʹka oblastʹ). I. Title.

DS135.U43L49 2014   940.53'1809224779   C2014-907572-3
                                                   C2014-907573-1

This is an original print edition of *Shattered Stones, Scattered Seeds*.

*Dedicated to my children, grandchildren
and the Neuringer mishpocha*

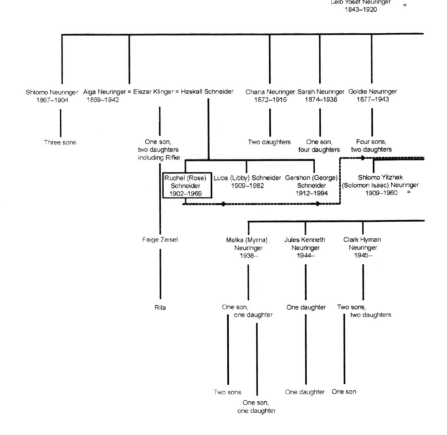

Leib Yosef Neuringer 1843–1920 =

Shlomo Neuringer 1867–1904 | Aiga Neuringer 1869–1942 = Elezar Klinger = Haskall Schneider | Chana Neuringer 1872–1916 | Sarah Neuringer 1874–1938 | Goldie Neuringer 1877–1943

Three sons | One son, two daughters including Rifke | Two daughters | One son, four daughters | Four sons, two daughters

Ruchel (Rose) Schneider 1902–1969 | Luba (Libby) Schneider 1909–1982 | Gershon (George) Schneider 1912–1994 | Shlomo Yitzhak (Solomon Isaac) Neuringer 1909–1960 =

Faige Zeisel | Malka (Myrna) Neuringer 1938– | Jules Kenneth Neuringer 1944– | Clark Hyman Neuringer 1945–

Rita | One son, one daughter | One daughter | Two sons, two daughters

Two sons | One son, one daughter | One daughter | One son

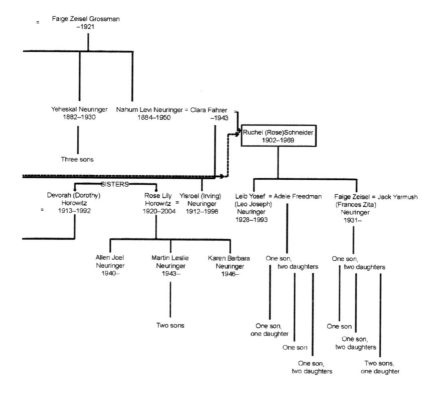

= Faige Zeisel Grossman
−1921

Yeheskal Neuringer
1882−1930

Nahum Levi Neuringer = Clara Fahrer
1884−1950   −1943

Ruchel (Rose)Schneider
1902−1969

Three sons

SISTERS

Devorah (Dorothy)
Horowitz
= 1913−1992

Rose Lily
Horowitz =
1920−2004

Yisroel (Irving)
Neuringer
1912−1998

Leib Yosef = Adele Freedman
(Leo Joseph)
Neuringer
1928−1993

Faige Zeisel = Jack Yarmush
(Frances Zita)
Neuringer
1931−

Allen Joel
Neuringer
1940−

Martin Leslie
Neuringer
1943−

Karen Barbara
Neuringer
1946−

One son,
two daughters

One son,
two daughters

Two sons

One son,
one daughter

One son

One son,
two daughters

One son

One son,
two daughters

Two sons,
one daughter

The study of history will never become obsolete, and a knowledge of one's grandfathers is an excellent introduction to history. Especially these grandfathers; they were a remarkable lot.

–*The World of Sholom Aleichem*, Maurice Samuel, 7.

[This book includes the *grandmothers* as well.]

Contents

"All happy families are alike, but an unhappy family is unhappy in its own way."
–Opening sentence from *Anna Karenina* by Leo Tolstoy

Prologue

It was *beshert.*[3]

Finding my paternal grandmother's story was meant to be. Almost a century after it happened, Clara Fahrer Neuringer's story, or at least her side of it, pushed its way out of the darkness of long-closed desk drawers, through the hesitant voice of the Yiddish translator and onto the starkly lit computer screen.

And now my brothers, cousins and I can mourn and weep for her lonely, misunderstood life.

We were always aware that there was a grandmother we were destined never to meet, but we knew little about her, neither how her voice sounded nor what she looked like, beyond the photograph that had a place of honor in our house.

The picture we had was a black-and-white portrait laminated onto a wooden frame, as was the custom in the late 1940s and 1950s; it stood on a table in our living room.

Grandma sits on a chair, hands resting one on the other on a table, facing toward the right. Her dark hair, with grey mixed through, is cut short, almost mannish in style, brushed off her face. She is middle-aged, with an unlined face; her eyes are clear.

And my late father looked exactly like her.

---

[3] Note: Words in italics are defined in the Glossary. Many common Yiddish words are not italicized after their first appearance.

Clara Neuringer – my grandmother

We knew our Grandpa Levi, our father's father, and his wife whom we called *Tante* Rosie. We knew they had two children, Uncle Leo and Aunt Fran, who were considerably younger than our father, Sol, and Uncle Irv, his younger brother.

It did not occur to us that this was a strange or unusual situation. After all, we had maternal grandparents. We had friends with no living grandparents, or just one or two. We felt fortunate to have a full complement, plus an extra *tante*.

2

This is what we knew. Clara Neuringer had lived and died in Borchov, the *shtetl* in Galicia where our fathers were born. She died – was killed – in October 1943. From the dim reaches of childhood memory, I call up a scene of my father sitting at the kitchen table of our apartment reading a letter that made him sad. "Grandma Clara died."

I was about six years old at the time, not an age when you would ask the pertinent, relevant questions that needed to be asked, should have been asked. Who wrote the letter? How did she die? The world was at war. How did a letter get out of a place occupied by the enemy? How long did it take for the letter to arrive at our apartment in Brooklyn, New York? It must have arrived after February 1944, when the older of my two brothers was born. He was not named for her.

But when my younger brother was born in August 1945, he was given the Hebrew name Chaim, after Chaya (Clara), our grandmother. Months later, Uncle Irv and Aunt Rose had a daughter who was named for her as well.

As the years went on, there were whispers that Grandma Clara did not die in a concentration camp; she had been shot to death. Our imaginations filled in the details. She was snared in a roundup. Or perhaps she was found hiding in the forest that surrounded Borchov.

Why hadn't she left Borchov and come to live in New York with our grandfather and our extensive extended family? Like the fourth son that we read about each year at the Passover *seder*, we were not wise enough to ask searching questions. Imagination once again filled in the blanks.

We knew that my father had returned to Borchov for six months in 1933. We had a photograph album recording that visit. We concluded that he had gone to try to convince

Grandma Clara to leave and travel back with him to New York. Because our father had returned alone, we concluded that Grandma didn't want to leave.

There were other, more furtive whispers that we overheard. These suggested that Grandma suffered from some kind of mental instability. As we grew older and began to learn more of the US immigration laws of the post–World War I period, the answers grew less definitive. Perhaps it wasn't that she wouldn't come; her mental condition might have barred her entry.

Beyond these basic details, there was much we did not know, both about her and about my father's childhood in Borchov.

We went on with our lives, growing up, passing through our teenage years into young adulthood. Marriage, careers, children followed, with no time to think about the woman in the picture. That picture always remained in a prominent place in both my father's and my uncle's homes.

Family mysteries don't disappear, however. They may recede from our awareness, but they remain waiting for someone to pick up the thread and begin to unravel the web.

Jews are commanded to remember their collective history as well as the ancestors who lived that history. Each year we repeat the cycle of rereading the *Torah* and reciting the *yizkor* prayer for departed family members.

By the end of the twentieth century, the meaning of yizkor had expanded to include a genre of books written in pain and sorrow by former residents of European towns and cities whose Jewish communities had been obliterated during the Holocaust. "Remember my family, friends, neighbors, my village, my way of life," these books plead.

For me, the journey began with the Yizkor Book, *Sefer Borchoff*, written in Yiddish and Hebrew and published in 1960

4

by a group of Borchovers who lived in Israel. Although I purchased a copy shortly after its publication, I couldn't read its contents. Since 1960 was also the year of my marriage, my move to Toronto and my beloved father's death, the book was placed on our bookshelf and ignored. There it languished, moving with us to our apartments and houses until January 2001, when I engaged Miriam Beckerman to translate sections of it.

Although I learned much of the life of the shtetl in general, there was little that could be related directly to my grandmother. What I was looking for specifically was whether there was an *Aktion* in October 1943, the supposed time of Clara's death.

Aktions were roundups of Jews or other "undesirable" residents undertaken by the occupying Nazis – shootings that occurred either in the town or the fields surrounding it. Jews from this area of Galicia were generally not transported to death camps, although there were forced labor camps in the area. But there were no major *Aktions* in 1943 that were mentioned in the Yizkor Book.

Then, in August 2006, Adele Neuringer gave me the manuscript of the family history my Grandfather Levi had written. Adele, widow of Leo, my father's half-brother, had found it while going through Leo's filing cabinet. It, too, was written in Yiddish. Once again I went to Miriam Beckerman to have it translated.

This memoir gave us an enormous amount of information about my grandfather's siblings and our great grandparents. But, incredibly, the memoir stops in mid-sentence, well before he recounts his marriage to Clara, the birth of his two sons and his leaving for New York.

The web was becoming more entangled with questions.

One other skein of threads to be unraveled was the collection of letters and postcards given to me in August 2011 by my cousin Martin Neuringer. Martin is the youngest son of Irv, my father's brother. The packet included receipts for money my grandfather had wired from New York to his parents and to Clara. Once again I began visiting Miriam Beckerman to have her unlock the stories that the fragile, folded letters and postcards told.

At the same time, another serendipitous moment occurred. Rifke, great granddaughter of my grandfather's oldest sister, Aiga, read the translation of the Yizkor Book I had posted on the JewishGen website. She was able to provide more details of my grandmother's life and death that she had heard from her mother.

The story the letters tell gives us only one side. It is as if we are overhearing a phone conversation; we do not know what the person on the other end is saying. There is an element of voyeurism in reading them. They were not meant to be read by a wider audience and we cannot fully understand the context in which they were written or who all the other people mentioned were.

Although the bulk of the letters were written by my Grandmother Clara in 1914, included in the packet were two letters written by my great grandfather, Leib Yosef Neuringer. These are particularly intriguing because they were written to explain (justify?) why my grandfather left Borchov when he did. Leib Yosef's tone is quite different from my grandmother's. The letters also present a different person from the one drawn by my grandfather in his memoir. Would the pious, much-loved, highly respected *melamed* of the memoir have dismissed his daughter-in-law as *meshuggah* with no thought of or concern for his very young grandsons left in her care?

My grandfather's memoir was written in hindsight, as a legacy for his children and grandchildren. My great-grandfather's letters were written in the moment, as were my grandmother's.

What follows is my attempt to weave together the tales from the three sources. We can only surmise what really happened.

The spelling of the town's name changed over time, depending upon the country it was in. It was spelled "Borszczow" when ruled by the Austro-Hungarian Empire and Poland. Today, as part of Ukraine, the town name is spelled "Borshchiv." To assist in pronounciation and for consistency, I've spelled it Borchov throughout.

Chapter 1:

Borchov in the Nineteenth Century

Borchov, the small village where the Neuringer and Fahrer families lived, is 98 kilometers or 61 miles southeast of Tarnopol. In this area of Eastern Europe, the Polish, Ukrainian and Austro-Hungarian Empire borders met and changed a number of times in response to changing political winds during the nineteenth and early twentieth centuries. This area, known as Galicia, had vast forests at that time. Nachman Blumenthal, the editor of the Yizkor Book, wrote that the town probably received its name from the *bór*, forest, that surrounded it.

Among Eastern European Jews, a village like Borchov is known as a shtetl. There were hundreds of such towns – some mere hamlets – that dotted the countryside of the Austro-Hungarian Empire, and the Czarist Russian Empire, which included most of today's Poland and Ukraine, an area known as the "Pale of Settlement."

Borchov never had a large population. According to the *Encyclopedia of Jewish Life*, the greatest number of people was reached during the 1890s when the total was 4,331, of whom 1,808 were Jews. This included Leib Yosef and Faige Zeisel Neuringer, our great grandparents, and their seven children. Here also lived the Fahrer family: Alter, his wife, Jute Hausner, and their children.

Blumenthal wrote that because the town was strategically located along several trade routes, it had probably been established in the Middle Ages. For example, goods were transported through Borchov en route from the larger city of

Tarnopol to Okip, which at that time was a fortress and trading center on the border of Poland, Russia and Romania. This trade route continued to Hatin and Yaz, in Turkey. There was another route that led north to Kiev in Ukraine.

The roads leading into and away from Borchov were unpaved, as were the streets and lanes within the shtetl itself. During the winter months these streets and roads were covered with ice and snow. During the other three seasons they could be either dry and dusty or muddy and slippery, depending upon the weather. Ruts formed by heavy wagon wheels were commonplace.

Among the people coming to Borchov were Jews. Blumenthal wrote that the first Jews probably arrived sometime during the sixteenth century. Jews were always seeking places where they could live quietly, peacefully, while following the tenets of their religion without undue interference.

The Polish noblemen who controlled the area at that time permitted Jews to stay in the town, but they were not allowed to buy any of the surrounding land.

While Borchov's strategic location brought trade, commodities and people to the village, it also brought armies on their way to occupy and conquer neighboring lands. And with each army came new laws, taxes, languages and currencies, imposing new burdens on the people.

The quality of life and well-being of the Jews rose and fell with the degree of tolerance displayed by successive occupiers. If occupiers were hostile to the Jews living in this area, pogroms would occur with no consequences for the peasants, many of whom were only too willing to aid in actually attacking the Jews.

In the Middle Ages, Borchov was part of Podolya, a province of Poland. During the 1600s there were many wars that led to the devastation of Poland by the Cossacks, the Tartars and the Russians. Even the Swedes sent armies to join in these invasions.

From 1672 to 1699, Turkey ruled Podolya, and Sultan Mehmed IV maintained a friendly policy toward the Jews. He let them settle wherever they wanted and abandoned all of the earlier restrictions.

This was a common and unsettling pattern of history that was repeated many times all over the continent. One ruler would welcome the Jews, followed by another who created a period of terror, death and destruction of the community. He in turn might be succeeded by yet another ruler exhibiting more tolerance. The security of the Jewish community depended upon the attitude of its rulers, who were always changing.

In 1699, Podolya, Borchov included, was returned to Poland. But the Polish monarchy was weak, and less than one hundred years later the country was split into pieces by the surrounding, stronger monarchies in Germany, Austria and Russia. In 1772, Galicia, and a large part of Podolya that included Borchov, was ceded to Austria. By 1795, Poland as a separate country had once again disappeared.

During the wars waged by the French General Napoleon Bonaparte, Borchov was taken over by the Russians (in 1809). I once asked my father why he had a number of books about Napoleon in our library, including Emil Ludwig's biography. Napoleon, my father declared, was his hero. I was astonished; I had been taught that Napoleon was a power-hungry general, trying to extend France's influence all across Europe.

My father went on to explain that as Napoleon's armies marched across Europe, they smashed the walls of the *ghettos* that had confined Jews.

After the defeat of Napoleon, the Congress of Vienna met in 1815 to redraw the map of the area. Galicia, including Borchov, was returned to the Austrian Empire. It remained there until after World War I, when, once again, it became part of Poland. Since the end of World War II, Borchov has been part of the Republic of Ukraine and is a quiet backwater with no Jews living within the town.

When telling people about Borchov, I usually say that my father was born in the Austro-Hungarian Empire but went to *gymnasium* in Poland, and were I to visit today, I would be traveling to Ukraine.

Chapter 2:
The Neuringer Family

In his memoir my grandfather wrote that when Leib Yosef Neuringer, my great grandfather, married Faige Zeisel Grossman, the bride chosen for him by his parents in 1856, he was thirteen and she was ten. They had not met before the wedding ceremony. Immediately afterward he returned to his parents' house and Faige Zeisel's parents took her home with them.

The reason given for this was that, from his palace in far-off Vienna, the Emperor, Franz Joseph I, had decreed that Jews would no longer be permitted to marry before the age of twenty-one. Since it was customary in those days for young Jewish people to marry in their mid-teens and begin to have children shortly thereafter, parents quickly arranged and registered marriages for their children of ten years and older before this new law came into force.

Such was life for the Jews living in Eastern Europe during the nineteenth and early twentieth centuries. They were constantly trying to balance following the laws and customs of their Jewish religion with obeying the harsh, often oppressive laws of a secular government far away. At the same time, they were living in small communities surrounded by people who were hostile to them.

The surname Neuringer is an unusual one and unique to this family whose origins were in Borchov. Wherever each Neuringer lives, all can trace their roots back to the same shtetl in Galicia. According to the *Dictionary of Jewish Surnames in Galicia*, "Neuringer" is a variant of "Neurong," which means renewal, regeneration and revival.

Leib Yosef and Faige Zeisel did what their parents demanded, for in the mid-nineteenth century few children living in the shtetls of Eastern Europe questioned the customs of their religion or the decisions made by their parents, certainly not at the ages of ten and thirteen.

According to the memoir, three years after the wedding ceremony, when Leib Yosef was sixteen and Faige Zeisel was thirteen, they began to live together as husband and wife. Their immediate worry was how Leib Yosef was going to make a living. His parents were very poor, and he had to find his own way to earn money. He had not been taught a trade nor had he developed a marketable skill. The only knowledge he had was from his religious schooling. His love of learning helped him decide to become a *melamed*.

When Leib Yosef began his teaching career, teachers were usually paid by each individual student. Since the majority of the people living in Borchov were poor, he would have received very little money for his efforts. Most likely, he accepted whatever the parents could pay rather than setting firm tuition fees or turning a student away.

In order to augment this meager living, Leib Yosef became a *baal tefillah* who would chant from the *bimah* in the synagogue on *Shabbos* and holidays. Faige Zeisel would proudly listen to him from her seat in the women's section of the synagogue as men and women did not (and still do not) sit together in the Orthodox synagogue.

Although being a *baal tefillah* brought in additional income, when Leib Yosef and Faige Zeisel began to have children a few years later, there was still not enough money for a growing family to live on.

Their first child, a son, was born in 1867. Faige Zeisel and Leib Yosef named him Shlomo. Two years later, a daughter whom they named Aiga, was born. Chana, the third child, was born in 1872.

Each time Leib Yosef and his growing family gathered around the table to eat, they began by saying a blessing over the bread. No matter how simple the meal – a bowl of soup, or bread and sliced vegetables – Leib Yosef would praise Faige Zeisel for her efforts to feed her large family. In his memoir, my Grandfather Levi, the youngest child, wrote how his father taught his children about his own poor childhood by describing the simple food his mother usually prepared. Leib Yosef recognized the arrival of a holiday by the soup his mother served. Most of the time, he told his children, his mother served a soup made with either barley or potatoes. But, on a *yontif*, the soup would have both barley and kasha (a buckwheat grain).

To augment their income, Faige Zeisel began to bake rolls and bread in her kitchen to sell to other women in the community. This enabled her to bring more money into the household while staying at home to care for her children.

More children were born: Sarah in 1874, followed three years later by Goldie, the youngest of the four Neuringer daughters. Since girls were expected to help their mothers at home, they could help her with the baking as they grew older.

As joyful as Faige Zeisel and Leib Yosef were with their growing, healthy family, they were also anxious. Girls were a particular burden in this culture. Suitable husbands needed to be found for them, and this meant saving enough money for sizeable dowries. The larger the dowry offered, the richer and more distinguished the prospective husband would be.

More sons were what Faige Zeisel and Leib Yosef prayed for, sons who could work outside the home and give a portion of their earnings to their parents.

Finally, in 1882 another son was born. They named him Yeheskal and made a huge feast at his *bris* with roasted meats and other delicacies. My grandfather commented in his memoir that it was the kind of meal that was usually served at a wedding.

The youngest of the seven children, Nachum Levi, was born on 23 December 1884. He was my grandfather. In his memoir he wrote that he was told when his mother was in labor she cried out: "Dear God, help me this last time and may I not have any more children thereafter."

His older brothers and sisters called him *dos mizinikal* (the youngest).

As the children grew old enough to assist Faige Zeisel in her business, she was able to add selling cereals and flour that her children could measure, weigh, bag and often deliver.

This was not an unusual turn of events. Many women of the shtetl worked, if not out of their houses as Faige Zeisel did, then running a stall in the market selling a variety of goods. Often the woman was the major wage earner in the family, as it was considered a real "catch" for a woman to marry a young man who would spend all his days studying Torah in the synagogue, even if it meant that she would be the primary source of financial support.

My grandfather wrote in his memoir that the members of Leib Yosef Neuringer's family were recognized in the community not only for their piety, but also for their hard work and their contributions and efforts to help those less fortunate than they.

However, life was never serene and stable for this growing family. Disease, death, political upheavals and wars affected Borchov and the Neuringer household. As their children grew and matured, joyful marches escorting sons and daughters to the marriage canopy alternated with processions to the cemetery to bury two of their children and a number of grandchildren. There were visits to the train station to say painful good-byes as children and grandchildren left Borchov to seek a better life in the New World. Often this meant that Leib Yosef and Faige Zeisel would never see them again.

The one constant Faige Zeisel and Leib Yosef had was their steadfast religious faith, the observance of which they maintained throughout their lives. Although we do not have a similar detailed account of my grandmother's family, I assume that Alter Fahrer and his wife faced similar experiences and challenges.

Chapter 3:

Clara and the Fahrer Family

Beyond the letters that Clara, her father, Alter Fahrer, sister, Jides Schneider, and father-in-law, Leib Yosef Neuringer, wrote and the sparse information we can glean from them, we do not have any memoir, diary or other record that can tell us more about the Fahrer family. We know that Clara's father was named Alter Fahrer from the letter that he wrote to my grandfather in New York in 1914.

In the Jewish Records Indexing–Poland database (JRI-Poland), I found an entry for a Chaje Beile Fahrer, born in 1881. Her father is listed as Alter Fahrer, her mother was Jute Hausner. Assuming this record is for my Grandmother Clara and that the information is correct, this suggests she was three years older than my grandfather.

Alter Fahrer and Jute Hausner's marriage is recorded as having taken place in 1885, when they were each forty-six years of age. This parallels the late listing of Leib Yosef's marriage to Faige Zeisel. Perhaps registrars were sent to Borchov in 1885-6 to update the records for census and tax purposes.

The same database shows four other children born to Alter Fahrer and Jute Hausner: Bincie Lea, Koppel, Shimon Eliyahu and Schidisi, all in the year 1886. Rather than interpret this to mean that these were quadruplets, I believe that the children were all registered with the authorities at the same time, regardless of their actual birthdates. This, apparently, was a not uncommon occurrence.

Confirming that these four children were Clara's siblings is her father's mentioning the two brothers in his postcard to my grandfather written after his wife's death. He wrote:

> Maybe you're upset with Chaiklen for convincing you to go to America. You should know that she figured that you are going to Koppel and that you will earn a living like Shimon Eliyahu. You would have a place to live with Shimon Eliyahu for $10 a week until you could get your own place and you would have room and board for very cheap.

We also know that Clara had a sister, Jides Schneider, to whom she was very devoted and who, in turn, was devoted to her and her children. On 24 June 1914, after a lengthy description of her loneliness and suffering, she wrote:

> But there is one thing that makes me very happy and that is I get along so well with Jides. She helped me very much and continues to help me with the dear children for whom she gives her whole life.

From all this I conclude that Clara had two brothers who emigrated to New York and two sisters.

There is, nevertheless, another mystery. Clara's brothers are Koppel and Shimon Eliyahu, but who was Leibl Fahrer, the author of the beseeching letter written on 2 March 1914, asking his father to go to the rebbe to seek prayers on behalf of his ill daughter? Alter Fahrer's postcard makes no mention of a sick grandchild. Yet Clara's postcard, written on 30 April, does say this:

> I've already written two letters to you at my brother's address. Because of the misfortune with Ruchel, you didn't get the letters.

Perhaps Koppel calls himself Leibl. Again, it is not uncommon to find people having Yiddish or Hebrew names, secular names, or nicknames. It is also possible that Leibl was born after 1886, the year when the older five children were registered.

Who exactly was Clara? Other than knowing what she looked like from the photograph that sat in a prominent place in our living room, we can only infer what her personal qualitites were from the letters she wrote and those that others wrote about her. Her father-in-law, Leib Yosef Neuringer, who called her "the Chaikela," paints a very negative picture of a woman with a fiery temper when he recounts to Yeheskal why Levi had to leave Borchov so precipitously. On 26 April, he wrote that "…she drove him out of the house immediately after *Purim*, to her brother, the rich guy, so what could we do…." A month earlier on 24 March, Leib Yosef had written to Levi that on the day he left "…[she] was still in a good mood and *farpitzed*. Whoever sees her says that she is *meshuggah*. Onc minute she is singing and the next minute she is crying."

These two qualities, that she liked to be well-dressed and that she had an unstable temperament, would cause serious consequences in the unfolding of her life story.

Although we do not know what education Clara received, we know that she was literate in Yiddish, at times poetic in her expression. She dates her letters using the Roman alphabet and Gregorian calendar. This is in contrast to her father, who dated his letter to my grandfather in Hebrew, using the name of the week's *Parsha* as the reference point.

Both Clara and her sister Jides signed their letters using the Roman alphabet, perhaps indicating that they were familiar with reading and writing in German. However, her last letters, written to my Uncle Irv in 1941, are signed with the diminutive, Chaiki.

Her constant references to God's help demonstrate her religious faith. However, her photograph shows that her head is uncovered and she is not wearing a wig. This would be congruent with the orthodox way my grandfather lived. None of the women in the extended Neuringer family wore wigs, nor did my grandfather wear a yarmulke outside of the synagogue. In contemporary terms, he would be called modern orthodox.

Since my father neither made mention of his maternal uncles living in New York, nor was there any contact with them or their children while we were growing up, or even today, we have no idea what they were like, what they did for a living, or what their families were like.

What we know of my grandmother and her family is limited to what she and they revealed in the letters we have.

Potatoes (Bulbes)[4]

Sunday - potatoes,

Monday - potatoes,

Tuesday and Wednesday - potatoes,

Thursday and Friday - potatoes,

The Sabbath brings a novelty - potato kugl!

Sunday, once more potatoes...

Chapter 4:
Faige Zeisel's Kitchen

People in Borchov, both Jews and non-Jews, ate foods that grew or were raised around them. The specific foods prepared by Faige Zeisel were often similar to those eaten by non-Jews for the simple reason that these were the foods grown or raised in the area. If the Polish or Ukrainian housewife took pride in her cabbage rolls, so did Faige Zeisel. The difference is that in her kosher house, she stuffed the cabbage with vegetables or beef and rice, never pork.

Faige Zeisel, her daughters and daughters-in-law also salted cabbages and turned them into sauerkraut, put cucumbers into brine to make pickles, and turned the plums from the orchards surrounding Borchov into plum jam, as did their non-Jewish neighbors.

---

[4] *Vishniac*, 2.

Friday was the busiest, most hurried day for Faige Zeisel and other Jewish housewives and still is today. In a traditional Jewish home like hers, all cooking and food preparation had to be completed before sundown and no cooking was done on *Shabbos* or a *yontif.*

Since Faige Zeisel baked bread and rolls for sale, she was up before dawn each day to fire up the brick oven with wood. Then she would prepare the dough, kneading and rolling it by hand. Once the oven was heated, the ashes had to be taken out before the bread could be put in. Her children could help her with this hot, dirty task.

The process was repeated several times until her orders were all filled. Only then could she prepare food for her own family. One of the products Faige Zeisel baked was the challah, the egg bread made with white flour that is eaten on Friday nights at the *Shabbos* meal and on other holidays and festivals.

There are different styles of challah. Most of the time Faige Zeisel braided the dough into an oblong shape that was wider in the middle, narrower at either end. For certain holidays, however, there were special shapes. The round challahs she baked at *Rosh Hashanah* symbolized the cycle of the year. Often, raisins were added to the dough at this time to suggest the hope for a sweet year.

When the last batch of challahs was placed in the oven to bake, Faige Zeisel would often prepare a *kugel.* This pudding was sometimes made with *lockshun,* sometimes with rice. During *Pesach,* when Ashkenazi Jews do not eat noodles or rice, a *kugel* would be made with mashed potatoes or matzo meal. In addition to the eggs that kept everything together, the ingredients varied. A *kugel* could be savory with fried onions, salt and pepper. At other times the *kugel* was sweet with sugar, cinnamon, sliced apples or dried fruit such as raisins.

Usually, she prepared one *kugel* for *Shabbos*, but if it was a special holiday, two different *kugels* were made. *Kugel* was such an important staple of the diet that there were proverbs about it. One had it that, "If you don't eat *kugel* for *Shabbos*, you'll go hungry all week." Another said that if someone ate *kugel* in the middle of the week, it meant that things couldn't be better for that person.

After the challah and *kugels* were removed from the oven, Faige Zeisel would often place a casserole containing a stew called *cholent* into the hot oven to bake slowly overnight. Because of the prohibition against cooking during *Shabbos* or on some festivals, *cholent* was developed to provide a warm *Shabbos* or *yontif* meal during the long, harsh winters. The stew was made mainly with dried beans and onions. If she had sold many rolls and challahs during the week and could afford it, the *cholent* might include some meat.

The intense heat of the oven would last long enough to cook the stew slowly and to keep it warm overnight. This long, slow period of cooking would actually improve its flavor.

On *Shabbos*, along with most families they knew, Faige Zeisel, Leib Yosef and their children would go to the synagogue in the morning and return home to eat the *cholent* for the mid-day meal.

In some households, if the mother didn't bake on Friday, or didn't have an oven large enough to hold the *cholent* casserole, she could take it to the village baker. She would pay him a few coins, and he would place the dish in his oven to cook overnight. After the *Shabbos* services it was common to see women hurrying to the baker's shop to retrieve the *cholent* and rushing home to serve it before it cooled off.

If times were good, the family would eat chicken on Friday nights. Faige Zeisel would choose the live chicken at the butcher's stall in the market on Thursday. The chicken would then be slaughtered according to the prescribed tradition by a *shoichet*, a man trained in the ritual killing of animals by slitting their throats quickly.

Even better times allowed Faige Zeisel to buy some meat from the butcher in the market. All the organs of the cow were eaten: liver, lungs, brains, tongue, kidneys – I have fond memories of eating some of these during my childhood.

After her daughter Goldie married Mendl Gross, a butcher, in 1897, Faige Zeisel no doubt obtained her meat from her son-in-law.

During the week, meals were much simpler. Breakfast would be a thick slice of bread or a roll spread with jam. They drank tea because milk was both costly and hard to keep in a house without refrigeration. There might be yogurt or soft, unripened cheese.

The boys would carry their lunches to *cheder* in a pail. They would find once again, bread, jam and perhaps an apple. Only at supper would the family eat a hot meal of soup or stew made with potatoes, carrots, onions or dried beans.

Each holiday had some special foods associated with it. On *Rosh Hashanah*, which comes in early fall, apples from local orchards were sliced and dipped in honey to bring a sweet year. Honey cakes were baked at this time as well.

At *Succos*, which is a holiday celebrating the harvest and comes shortly after *Rosh Hashonah*, Faige Zeisel would often prepare stuffed cabbage, cabbage soup or stuffed green peppers.

Hanukkah comes in late November or December and reminds Jews of the small amount of oil the Maccabees found in the destroyed temple in Jerusalem. The miracle of the oil lasting for eight days is remembered by eating latkes, pancakes made of grated potatoes and fried in oil.

Before Purim, an early spring holiday, Faige Zeisel baked different kinds of sweets, which she would put in baskets and take to neighbors and friends. She always included triangular cakes called *hamantashen.* These were filled with poppy seeds or a jam made from prunes. The triangular shape was to remind everyone of the hat that Haman, the villain of the Purim story, wore.

Preparation for Pesach, a spring holiday, meant a thorough cleaning of the household. To ensure that no bread crumbs remained in the house during Pesach, Faige Zeisel's daughters Aiga, Chana, Sarah and Goldie helped their mother completely scour it and take out the special plates, pots, pans and cutlery that were exclusively used for the eight days of the holiday.

Matzo, thin and crisp like a cracker and baked no more than eighteen minutes, is eaten throughout the eight days of Pesach. Some families less fortunate than Faige Zeisel's ate only meat or fish during the holiday because it was too expensive to have two sets of dishes (one for meat, one for dairy) set aside for Pesach use only. In the Yizkor Book, one Borchover is quoted as declaring each year, "Who needs to eat cheese during Pesach?"

Forty days after Pesach, *Shavous* is celebrated. This holiday has two meanings. On the one hand it is another harvest holiday, celebrating the spring harvest in Israel. On the other hand, the holiday also recalls the giving of the Torah to Moses at Mount Sinai. Dairy dishes, especially those made with cheese, are eaten at the time to remind Jews of the night spent waiting for Moses to return from the mountain. Faige Zeisel traditionally made blintzes or cheesecakes for this holiday.

All of her recipes were transported in the memories of the immigrants to the New World and lovingly recreated. I have tasty recollections of feasting on the *knishes*, *kugels*, borschts, meats and sweet treats that my mother, maternal grandmother and Neuringer relatives prepared in their New York kitchens. The fact that today many of these foods are considered "off limits" because of modern health and dietary concerns makes the memory of them all the more mouthwatering!

Chapter 5:
Making a Living

When members of the Neuringer and Fahrer families and other Borchovers began leaving Borchov between the end of the nineteenth century and the outbreak of World War I, they did so mainly for economic reasons. How, then, had they earned their livings before they departed? From the Yizkor Book, a picture emerges of a society pressured by the changes brought about by the industrial revolution, a pressure compounded by the specific restrictions placed upon the Jewish community.

Most of the Jews of Borchov were tradespeople, buying and selling goods that were brought into the village. Some were craftspeople making leather goods or items of tin or cloth. They came to these callings by default. From the time of Polish rule in the Middle Ages, when the first Jews most likely arrived and settled in the area, Jews were not permitted to own land.

Based on the description of economic life in the Yizkor Book written by Nachman Blumenthal, Borchov appears to have been a self-sufficient community centered around its market. The market was a bustling, busy place where people bought and sold food and all the goods they needed for daily life; it was also the place for the meeting of friends and for entertainment, the place where special events were held.

It is possible that, while growing up, the Neuringer and Fahrer children might have thought that if their mother could not find something in the market, it did not exist anywhere. From fruits and vegetables in season; to eggs, butter, cheese, beef, chicken and fish; to staples such as salt, sugar, and flour, Faige

Zeisel could find everything she needed to cook the family's meals. Twice a year, before Rosh Hashanah and Pesach, if Faige Zeisel could afford it, she would buy some cloth to make new dresses for her daughters. If she could not, they hoped she would at least purchase new hair ribbons for them.

When they needed new shoes, Faige Zeisel took them to the cobbler, who made shoes and boots. The area around his stall was redolent with the smell of new leather. Making one's own clothes or having clothes made to order continued until World War I. In his letter to my grandfather on 26 April 1914, Leib Yosef wrote that Clara had a suit made by Moshe Stoller and "purchased everything, even the boots."

Near the cobbler's shop was one where saddles for horses were made. Since few people had horses and fewer still needed new saddles, the saddle maker also made bags, belts and other items of leather to sell.

On a Thursday, the busiest day, or before a *yontif*, there were one or two men who stood in the middle of the market waiting for someone to hire them to carry heavy packages. They were known to be able to hoist a sack of flour weighing over two hundred pounds on their shoulders and carry it for quite a distance. They were paid a few coins for this. I picture Yeheskal, who was known to play hooky from his *cheder* classes, wandering in the market, following the porter to his destination and occasionally being rewarded by watching an argument break out between the porter and the one who hired him. The disagreement was always over the same thing. The porter expected to get more money than the one who hired him was willing to pay!

There were Borchovers who owned horses and wagons; they were hired to take people to and from the train station or to neighboring shtetls. Sometimes they were hired to deliver heavy items such as a new stove or a cabinet from the carpenter's shop to a house for an agreed-upon price. There was no set amount charged for these services. Each arrangement had to be individually negotiated. The way of the market was to haggle over the price and bargain to get the most while paying the least. Most of the time, this was carried on with good humor.

Women were active participants in this market economy. Some, such as my great grandmother, who baked bread and rolls, worked out of their homes. Women who were seamstresses and hairdressers were others who could easily work from their homes.

It is possible that my grandparents followed this custom of having their business and residence in the same building. From the descriptions in her letters, it seems as if the living and working quarters were combined.

When Faige Zeisel and Leib Yosef were children, there were people in the shtetl who made soap; there were others who made wax candles. By the time their children grew up, such items were manufactured in the large cities, and people bought them in the stores in the market.

The same thing was happening to items made of tin, such as locks, baking pans and candle sticks. More and more people were looking to buy tin goods that were factory manufactured rather than handmade.

Blacksmiths who made shoes for horses or iron wheels for wagons, clock makers and those who made clay pots or containers were all skilled people who found their jobs were disappearing as more and more goods that were manufactured elsewhere became available in the shtetl market.

When possible, some of the families who had been in these trades began to move to the larger cities, such as Lvov or even Warsaw, where they could use their skills working in the factories. However, there were often restrictions on the numbers of Jews who could move to the urban areas.

Not all Borchovers bought and sold goods. In addition to people such as Leib Yosef who were *melameds,* there were those who had other skills.

One couple, Raisa and Alter Blumenthal[5] were glaziers. They put glass windowpanes into new homes and repaired broken ones. Alter learned this trade from his wife, Raisa, whose father had taught her. Nachman Blumenthal remarked that Raisa always did a better job than her husband.

Chaim Wolfinger[6] and members of his family built houses. They did this without following any blueprints and without any assistance from architects. They hired a crew of non-Jewish workers – some were Polish; others were Ukrainian. These men were all experienced in constructing private houses or shops. They could estimate how much brick, wood or sand was needed for the project. One such worker was a Jew named Shmuel Melamed.[7] He would use his belt to measure how much sand was needed for the area.

Even though none of these men had formal training, the buildings they erected lasted for many generations. Blumenthal pointed out, however, that the walls were not always straight, and the floors not always level.

---

[5] Note: These were actual Borchovers.

[6] ibid.

[7] ibid.

Even after my grandfather's eldest brother, Shlomo and his wife, Batya, closed their grocery store, which had not provided them with much of a livelihood, and he trained to become a bookbinder, it was still a struggle to maintain that business and earn enough to support a family. Shlomo was required to purchase a license to open his bookbinding shop and had to renew it yearly. Another reason for economic hardship was the high taxes that the merchants had to pay to the government.

There were creative Borchovers who found a way out of this dilemma. Since Borchov was close to both the Russian and Romanian borders, smuggling became a successful way of life for them. Nachman Blumenthal remembered that some smugglers were very well known in Borchov for their abilities to bring in manufactured goods, whisky, or even young Jewish boys who were trying to avoid being drafted into the Czar's army in Russia. Smuggling even created new jobs. Men were hired as guides to point the way through the forests, and others worked as porters to carry the goods. Blumenthal believed that the Jewish population of Borchov actually grew before World War I because of this flourishing new "business," while in the nearby shtetls, the population went down as more and more people left.

Not all of the Jews worked in the markets of the shtetl. In some areas, the *porets*, the Polish noblemen who owned forested land, would lease land to a Jew who then had the right to cut the trees on the land for lumber. There were a few Jews who rented small plots of land and raised some animals and crops.

Yeheskal, the second of Faige Zeisel and Leib Yosef's sons, wanted to be one of them. He was not interested in studying as his brother had, nor did he have the same ability to learn. My grandfather wrote that despite his *melamed's* attempts to teach him the *aleph-bet*, or to chant the prayers, the lessons did not "stick."

Yeheskal preferred being outdoors. He watched enviously as non-Jewish boys and girls who lived outside Borchov brought chickens, geese, goats and cows to the market. He looked at the baskets of apples, plums, cucumbers, peppers, potatoes, carrots and cabbages set up at the market stalls and thought about the fields where they grew.

In the summer when Yeheskal and his friends went swimming in the narrow Nichtawa River at the edge of the shtetl, he looked longingly at the fields on the other side.

One day he announced to Faige Zeisel and Leib Yosef that he wanted to be a farmer. He dreamed of renting an orchard from a nobleman and growing apples and plums. Perhaps he would buy a cow or two for her milk, which he would sell in Borchov. He yearned to have chickens or even a goat living in a small area next to his house. But the people who rented land lived on the outskirts of Borchov, not on farms. Besides, it would take a large amount of money to rent an orchard or buy a cow.

His mother and father were shocked and dismayed to hear of Yeheskal's ambition. Jews could not own land; they were not farmers.

In spite of the changes taking place and the economic hardships most Borchovers encountered, there were some who appeared to make a comfortable living. One such person was Mendl Gross, who married my grandfather's sister Goldie. He was a butcher.

Mendl Katzev (Gross)

According to my grandfather's memoir, another brother-in-law, Archie Kowalek, was able to provide Sarah with all that she needed, including a maid to assist her with household chores and raising their children. However, my grandfather did not explain what Archie did.

Two jobs remained unchanged right up until the outbreak of World War II. One was the bathhouse keeper. Since there was no indoor plumbing in Borchov, men and women went to the bathhouse to bathe. Women usually went to the *mikvah* that was supervised by the rabbi and used for ritual purposes. Men went to an ordinary bathhouse. The job of the bathhouse keeper

33

was to heat the ovens that in turn heated the water. He was paid by each man who used the bath. He would also get some more money for lending the bather a whisk broom that was made from the willow branches used to make *lulavs* at *Succos*. Bathers used these brooms to wipe off their perspiration.

The man who ran the bathhouse was considered the lowest level of worker in the Jewish community. There was even a saying that reflected this: "From the *rov* to the bath man."

The other occupation that remained unchanged through the years was that of the water carrier. This was someone who filled barrels with water from the river each day and loaded them onto a horse-drawn wagon. Then he would walk through the shtetl, going from house to house, delivering water for drinking and cooking. He was paid a few pennies for each jug of water.

Years after the end of World War II, Nachman Blumenthal described one of Borchov's water carriers in the *Book of Borchoff*.

> Yosef Hirsh was one of the water carriers. [He] transported the water in barrels and he always had half dead horses [to pull the wagon]. The horses strained and suffered before they could bring the water from the Dalina River.
>
> He loved Yiddish papers and after he would get paid for the two cans of water, he would ask for a newspaper. He didn't care what date the paper was printed. He liked to read at home after work. He couldn't speak very well, but when he read the paper, his wife would sit by his side and *shep naches* from her man. If he managed to say a whole word, such as "fire" or figure out the headlines, he was happy. He would read one word and say, "Do you hear?" And his wife would reply, "*Oy vay is mir.*"

She was very proud of her husband and told her neighbors that all Jewish wives should have such a man.

In the winter the whole wagon, especially the wheels, was all covered with snow and ice, and the wheels screeched, so that you could hear the wagon coming from several streets away.

From the distance you could [also] hear Yosef Hirsh screeching. His face was wrapped with a shawl. His horse pulled a wagon that had two wooden barrels that hung from both sides. He was pleading with the horse to pull the water up the hill, and when he couldn't get the horse to do this peacefully, he hit him with his whip. Generally, Yosef Hirsh tried his best not to hit the horse too hard. He used to say that you have to have pity on an animal; you shouldn't plague him too much.

Yosef Hirsch

A Jew must study Torah all he can,

Not bother with what's light and foolish,

For praised be he who honors God and man,

Both earns a living and is studious.[8]

Chapter 6:
Education

I picture a dark December morning in 1888, days after Levi's fourth birthday. Leib Yosef returns home after saying his morning prayers, instead of proceeding on to the *cheder* where he taught. Levi waits for him, dressed in his *yontif* clothes. This was the day that Levi would begin to attend *cheder*, the traditional way of educating boys in the shtetl.

I see father and son leaving the house and walking along the narrow cobblestone streets to the nearby school. In one hand, Leib Yosef holds a basket covered with a cloth napkin. In it are sweets – raisins, nuts, cookies – that Faige Zeisel has prepared especially for this joyous occasion.

Once in the small school building, Levi is warmly welcomed by the *melamed* and his assistant, the *belfer*. The other boys – for *cheder* was only for boys – are laughing and chattering, delighted to have a break from their regular lessons. Perhaps Yeheskal, Levi's older brother, was there as well.

---

[8] *From the Poem "Motl" by Mordecai Gebertig (1877 - 1942), Vishniac, 34.*

The *melamed* settles everyone down, places a book in front of Levi and opens it to the first page. Leib Yosef takes a small jar of honey from the basket and spills a small drop of it onto the page.

Instinctively Levi puts his finger on the honey, and then licks it. "Aahh," everyone cries, "*mazel tov.*"

Levi had just completed his first lesson: learning is sweet. Leib Yosef then distributed the tiny cookies and sweets that were in the basket. He hurried off to his own class that was waiting for him, while Levi's *melamed* went back to teaching his boys the letters of the Hebrew alphabet, the *aleph-bet*.

And so Levi's school days began. The next day the *belfer* came to his house to escort him and the other young boys in his class to school. Levi carried a small pail that held his lunch of bread, jam and fruit that Faige Zeisel prepared for him. The *belfer* brought him back home in the early evening.

Shlomo and Yeheskal had begun their education in the same celebratory way. Their curriculum was a religious one. For the "People of the Book," it was paramount to learn to read Hebrew so they could read their prayer book and the Torah, the five books of Moses. As the boys grew older, they would learn and study the *Mishnah Torah*, the commentaries.

The story was different for their sisters Aiga, Chana, Sarah and Goldie and the other young girls living in shtetls, such as my Grandmother Clara. When her daughters began school, Faige Zeisel did not pack a basket of special sweets as she had when her sons entered the *cheder*. There was no special ceremony to welcome them. Their school day was shorter than the boys'. Their *melamed* might not have been as learned as the *melamed* in a boys' *cheder*.

Occasionally the girls' teacher was the wife of the *melamed* or rebbe. She would teach the girls the *aleph-bet* so that they could read some prayers in the prayer book. But once they learned those prayers, the rest of their instruction would be in Yiddish. They would learn to read a Yiddish version of the Torah, known as the *"Tsene-rene,"* that was written in the Middle Ages expressly for women.

Upon their return home, the sisters were expected to help Faige Zeisel with household chores. Each one had responsibilities in caring for a younger sister or brother and helping her mother with her baking business. At the same time, Faige Zeisel was teaching her daughters to sew and cook and how to organize and run a Jewish household.

School, whether for boys or girls, was not free, and the number of years a child stayed there often depended upon the economic situation of the parents. Sometimes, as in Yeheskal's case, it was the student who resisted the hours spent in school. Even a young child might seek ways not to have to be in a classroom.

My grandfather described one such episode that occurred when he was four or five years old. Among his earliest memories was his sense that Faige Zeisel and Leib Yosef believed him to be physically weak, in need of coddling at times. One morning when the *belfer* arrived to walk him to *cheder*, Levi announced that he had a headache. The truth was that he hated going to school.

Leib Yosef believed Levi, however, so Levi remained home that day, staying in the warmth of the kitchen, watching Faige Zeisel and his sisters bustle about baking and selling to the women who came to the house.

The next day when the *belfer* arrived once again, Levi turned pale with guilt. Immediately Leib Yosef ran up to him and asked: "My dear son, is your head hurting you again?"

Before he could answer Faige Zeisel interrupted, *"Melamed*, why are you telling him he has a headache? Don't you see that he is pale because of the *belfer*? He does not want to go to school."

Leib Yosef shouted back, "How can you be so mean, don't you see that the child is sick?""

But his mother had had enough of his acting sick; Levi went off to school. Faige Zeisel had seen how Yeheskal, her second son, had shown his disinterest in going to *cheder*, and she was not going to allow this to happen a second time.

Levi was not like his older brother, however. As he progressed to higher levels of Jewish studies and had more qualified teachers, his excellence as a student became apparent. *Melameds* in *cheders* did not write formal report cards at that time. His teachers would informally report to Leib Yosef that Levi had a "good head" – that he quickly absorbed his lessons and was able to understand the finer points of subtle Talmudic arguments.

To find out just how good a student Levi was, Leib Yosef arranged for one of the best *melameds* in Borchov to test him. My grandfather did not write how old he was when this took place, but I imagine that it occurred around the time that his *bar mitzvah* was approaching. It was time to decide if he would continue his education or begin to work. The examination was an oral one, with Levi having to reply to questions of text and give interpretations of the Torah that the *melamed* presented to him.

The day after the examination, the *melamed* met with Leib Yosef and gave him a report, also oral, evaluating how Levi performed. Faige Zeisel and Levi anxiously waited at home for Leib Yosef's return. He came into the house, wordlessly patted

Levi on the cheek and then went over to Faige Zeisel, quietly whispering in her ear. Levi watched her face closely; as she listened he could see a wide smile spread across her face and her eyes sparkle with pride. It was then that Levi understood what the pat on the cheek meant. His examination results were "First Class."

From then on there was no doubt that Levi would remain in the *cheder* until his *bar mitzvah*. Unfortunately, my grandfather's formal education ended shortly after that. Economic necessity trumped scholarly interest or ability.

When Yeheskal, Levi's older brother, left Borchov for New York, Levi had to begin work to replace the money that his brother had contributed toward the running of the household. Years later, he wrote:

> ...they took me out of *cheder*, but they couldn't tear me away from studying, and in the evenings and on *Shabbos* I studied alone. Thursdays and *Shabbos* in the evenings I used to sit in the *Bais Ha-Medresh* with friends and study until four or five in the morning and then go home and go to work … In addition, when my eldest brother became ill and could no longer work at his bookbinding trade, I had to help him also. I remember early one Friday morning when I was returning home from the *Bais Ha-Medresh*, I saw it was lit up in his place. He had already awakened for work so I went in to him. He asked me, "Why did you get up so early?"
>
> I told him that I did not get up yet, because I had not gone to bed yet..."

Even if a boy from the shtetl was able to continue attending *cheder*, he still lacked a complete secular education. Although there was a state-run *gymasium* in Borchov,

40

attendance was not compulsory at that time, nor was it entirely free. Had a Jewish Borchov boy managed to graduate from *gymnasium*, however, his religion would have barred him from further study. Although there were excellent universities in Vienna, Krakow, Warsaw and other large Eastern European cities, some schools dating back to the Middle Ages, few would accept any Jews. Competition was very keen, making it even more difficult for an unsophisticated boy from a shtetl to be given a coveted place. This situation was even more restricted for women, who never received the same rigorous education, whether religious or secular, in the first place.

As the nineteenth century drew to a close, there was some loosening of the prejudicial barriers that created a quota system for Jewish students. Although women were beginning to attend European and North American universities and a few were entering professions in science and medicine, fewer still were Jewish. Such a quota system also existed in North American colleges and universities, but these were unofficial and not acknowledged officially.

Frustrated that their sons were unable to aspire to a profession, but valuing learning and study, Jews of Eastern Europe turned inward. Their sons became lifelong religious scholars. They would study, argue and deconstruct religious text in a *yeshivah* – a school of higher religious learning – for as long as possible. Some parents arranged marriages for their sons to girls whose families could support them while the son continued to study. In other cases, the wife ran a shop or stall in the market while her husband studied.

In most cases, attending a *yeshivah* was not possible, so the young man would work during the day and study two or three evenings a week in the *Bais Ha-Medresh*. It was this path that Faige Zeisel and Leib Yosef chose for their sons.

Having overcome his early childhood resistance to *cheder*, Levi was determined that his sons should follow the traditional path. Throughout the remainder of his life he promoted both secular and religious schooling. Even though he was living in New York, he must have written about his concern that his son, Shlomo, begin his *cheder* studies. The start of Shlomo's schooling was delayed because of the death of Clara's mother. Clara's father, Alter Fahrer, wrote a postcard to Levi informing him of this: "Shlomtzi didn't start learning *Chumash* yet because it was a few weeks before [arrangements were made]. After that he will start." Therefore, my father did not begin attending *cheder* until the summer of 1914, two months after his fifth birthday.

In her postcard dated 11 August 1914, Clara wrote, "Now, my dear husband, I can tell you that our sweet son, may he be well, is growing with *mazel*. He started this Sunday to learn *Chumash*."

Did Clara send a basket of sweets to accompany my father's first day of *cheder*, as Faige Zeisel had done for Shlomo's father, Levi, before him?

Chapter 7:
Seeking the Rebbe's Advice

Shlomo, born in 1867, was my grandfather's eldest brother. In his memoir my grandfather wrote this of him:

> He received a very strict Orthodox upbringing and studied with all the greatest of the *melamedim*. He was, as people used to say in those times, a child who loved to learn. In addition to his spiritual characteristics, he was very handsome physically. He had a good nature and was loved by everyone.

As Shlomo approached manhood he was confronted with the difficult decision of how he would make a living in Borchov. As many young men of his era did, Shlomo left his full-time studies that were basically religious and did not prepare him for a career. There were few opportunities in Borchov for a studious Jewish boy to receive a secular education, fewer still for a Jewish student to attend university. In addition to the high cost, there were strict quotas. A young man from a small provincial village stood little or no chance to be admitted.

My grandfather wrote what happened:

> He married a girl from a very aristocratic family. They essentially "bought" him because he was such a worthy fellow.

Shlomo Neuringer and Batya Steinig married in 1888. It is likely that Batya's parents provided the funds for them to open a grocery store. When the business did not provide enough of a living to support a family, Shlomo trained to be a bookbinder.

Their first child, a boy whom they named Isaac, was born around 1890. I can imagine the joy and celebration that resounded through the Leib Josef Neuringer extended family; Isaac was the first of many grandchildren that were expected to follow. Shmuel Nusen was born in 1891, and Batya delivered a third son, Herman, in 1894.

Alas, the joyous sounds of a household busy with raising children in health and happiness were muted that same year when a cholera epidemic swept through Borchov and the surrounding area. Cholera, caused by unsanitary conditions, was a frequent visitor to all communities in those days. Isaac, the beloved first-born son and grandson was one of its victims, succumbing to the disease at age four years and nine months.

Batya continued to bear children. The database on JRI-Poland shows that Mariem Lea, who was born in 1896, lived for only nine months. The following year, 1897, Chaim Mordko was born and a second daughter, Beila Ruchel, was born in 1900.

Death, however, continued to claim Shlomo and Batya's infants. Beila Ruchel lived for only seven months, while Chaim Mordko was three and a half when he died in 1901.

My grandfather did not write whether Shlomo and Batya sought out a medical explanation for these early deaths; it is possible that no doctor was available. It is more likely that contemporary medical knowledge did not provide prevention or treatment.

His grief inconsolable, his anger uncontained, Shlomo did what many in Borchov would have done: he sought out a rebbe's advice. Unlike the modern rabbi, whose honorific comes after rigorous study in an accredited religious institution, in the shtetl the rebbe was recognized as a *tzaddik* or wise man, whose reputation was derived from both his knowledge of the texts and the quality of the advice that he gave his adherents.

Not all shtetls had a rebbe living within the village. If there was not a local one, those who could would travel to the nearest shtetl where a rebbe of considerable reputation lived. Other times, a rebbe would travel from one shtetl to another dispensing his wisdom.

Shlomo Reibel, who wrote the chapter "How They Spent Their Leisure Time" for the Yizkor Book, described what "a great event" it was when a rebbe came to visit Borchov. Young boys dressed in their best clothes and riding horses with bells on their harnesses would wait at Borchov's outskirts. There they would meet the young men who accompanied the rebbe from the shtetl he had previously visited, and the escorting responsibilites would be handed over to the Borchovers. Sometimes local Chassidim hired a horse and wagon so that they, too, could join the parade of people leading the rebbe to the house where he was to stay during his visit.

Upon his arrival, crowds of people would begin streaming to the house, each with his or her personal petition. In addition to posing questions for interpretation of religious practice, there were requests for special prayers for a sick child or other relatives, pleas for work or for assistance in solving marital discords or business disagreements. Each petitioner gave the rebbe a donation according to his or her means in return for the rebbe's answer.

Reibel wryly noted, "Very rare was it that anyone in the shtetl, while the rebbe was there, had the courage to be a non-believer."

Whether Shlomo traveled outside of Borchov to seek advice or went to a visiting rebbe or to a Borchov resident is irrelevant. The important thing is that, distraught over the deaths of his babies and unable to understand why they were dying, Shlomo challenged the rebbe to tell him why God poured his whole wrath on him.

Even today it is not unusual to find clergy giving solace and comfort to those living with medical traumas or to those in mourning. Chaplains visit the sick in hospitals, and medical facilities provide areas for prayer or quiet contemplation. It is not uncommon to call upon religious faith to augment scientific practice. If answers cannot be found in one realm, perhaps they are in another.

If Shlomo's going to the rebbe was not unusual, the rebbe's answer certainly was. My grandfather reported:

> The rebbe promised Shlomo that he would pray to God for him, and when Shlomo's wife would become pregnant again he should let the rebbe know and at the proper time [the rebbe] would give a name for the newborn child.

Shortly after, Batya became pregnant and delivered another girl. As instructed, Shlomo returned to the rebbe, who named the infant Batsheva.

My grandfather wrote in his memoir that the rebbe told Shlomo, to "return home and give the mother a *mazel tov*, and tell her that Batsheva is mine with long years."

Thus the wrath of God was to be diverted from Batsheva if God believed she belonged to the rebbe rather than Shlomo.

The rebbe's plan failed. Batsheva was seven months old when she died in 1902. Shlomo's grief yet again could not be consoled, and his cry was bitter as he claimed that Batsheva carried half his heart with her to the grave. Nevertheless Batya became pregnant one last time and a son, Mattityahu, was born in 1903.

All this misfortune took its toll on Shlomo's health, which began to fail after he contracted tuberculosis, another incurable scourge of the era. He went to a sanatorium, hoping that the crisp, clear mountain air would cure him. He was only thirty-seven when he died in 1904. Batya died shortly afterward, consumed by her grief.

Of the eight children that Batya bore, only three, all sons, survived into manhood. In his memoir, my grandfather did not record who raised the three boys after their parents died. If they did not join the household of Leib Yosef and Faige Zeisel, perhaps they became part of their mother's family.

The eldest, Shmuel, was conscripted to fight during World War I. In spite of being wounded, he returned to Borchov after the war, married and had children.

His two younger brothers, Herman and Mattityahu, emigrated to New York where they married and had families, whose descendants live there now. Once in New York the two brothers became part of the large, extended Neuringer family of cousins. I remember seeing them, their wives and daughters (neither had sons) at family gatherings and *simchas*.

My grandmother's brother, Leibl Fahrer, also turned to his rebbe in Borchev during a time of extreme emotional pain. He was living in New York with his wife and six children. On 2 March 1914, Leibl wrote a four-page letter to his father, Alter, in Borchov.

> We've already endured a lot in America ... now ... I'm writing with tears and pain ... You should go immediately to the rebbe and tell him everything about our misfortune.

Leibl goes on to describe his daughter:

> [My] precious daughter, Ruchel, has gotten a cold and suffers very badly from it with high fever and headaches, and it's already four weeks and nothing seems to help ... Now she's confined to bed, so pray for her, dear father.
>
> I would give my whole fortune if only God would restore good health to the dear child. I don't have patience to write. May God help; I've done everything I can.

Earlier he had written that "....money is going so quickly – a $100 – may it bring good results." Presumably this $100 came from medical assistance. Having exhausted all the means of assistance in New York, he added a postscript to his letter:

> I'm sending you 40 kroners ... dear father, go immediately to the rebbe and tell him everything about my misfortune. And may God have mercy and grant relief from our troubles.

The writing in the last paragraph of the letter is unclear; all Miriam Beckerman could discern is that he had already spent $2000, an enormous amount of money at that time, on attempting to have his sick child treated. Even without being able to read the complete paragraph, this father's plaintive cry for help for his child resonates across the century.

Chapter 8:

A Century Ends

During the last decades of the nineteenth century, Faige Zeisel and Leib Yosef needed to turn their attention from caring for and educating small children to preparing them for adult life.

Shlomo, the eldest, was the first to marry. In the previous chapter, I quoted from my grandfather's memoir regarding the sizeable dowry my great grandparents received from Shlomo's wife's family. When Faige Zeisel and Leib Yosef arranged for their eldest daughter Aiga to marry Elezar Klinger, who had also been born in Borchov, they needed to provide a dowry for her.

Daughters were considered a mixed blessing in a Jewish household. On the one hand, Faige Zeisel surely would have been delighted to have four daughters who could help her with the baking and the sales of flour and grains. On the other hand, as the girls grew old enough to get married, Leib Yosef might have agreed with Sholom Aleichem's fictional character Tevye that many daughters were a burden as much as a joy.

The more generous the dowry, the more suitable the candidate for marriage would be. Unfortunately, by the time their four daughters were of marriageable age, Faige Zeisel found her business income had diminished because of hard times, and the family actually went into debt to pay for the dowries and weddings.

Aiga was twenty when she married. Although my grandfather did not specify how Elezar earned his living, he noted that it was a good one.

Aiga and Elezar had three children: Harry, Mindel and Rivka. When Elezar developed an unspecified illness, my grandfather's quaint description was that "the sun stopped shining" on this happy household. A few years later Elezar died at a relatively young age, leaving Aiga to raise their three young children on her own.

Desperate to make a living to support her family, Aiga decided to do what her mother had done years before: bake bread and rolls for sale. Aiga probably chose baking because it was familiar – Aiga had assisted her mother until she married Elezar. Times had changed, however. There were bakers who had opened stores in the market. Some of the younger women in Borchov preferred buying their bread and rolls from these professionals. In the house, all the work still had to be done by hand, and although it was good to have the oven going all day to heat the house in the winter, in the summer it was stifling.

After struggling for a few years, Aiga realized that she could not earn an adequate living and felt that she had no choice but to accept the suggestion to marry again.

It would not have been an easy task for the matchmaker to find a husband willing to marry a poor widow with three young children to feed, clothe and care for. Haskall Schneider, a gentle man, became Aiga's second husband. Within a few years they had two daughters of their own, Ruchel, born in 1902, and Liba, born in 1909.

While they were deeply concerned about Aiga's difficulties, Faige Zeisel and Leib Yosef had many other worries. Foremost among these was saving enough money for three more dowries.

Chana presented a particularly difficult challenge to Faige Zeisel. When she was seven years old, Chana fell ill with a severe illness, and although she survived, her right side was left paralyzed for the rest of her life. Once again, my grandfather did not name what caused this, but rheumatic fever, polio or meningitis are among the possibilities, all of which can now be prevented with vaccines or treated with antibiotics.

In spite of the grief everyone in the family would have felt, both parents and Chana were determined that she lived as normal a life as possible. Instead of being relegated to a corner of the household, as was done with so many others at that time, she was encouraged to participate in family activities as much as she was able.

Although she was unable to cook or write, she learned to read, proving that her ability to reason and think was not affected by her illness. She would greet customers who came into the house and sell them the bread, rolls and grains they needed. My grandfather recalled that her greetings were warm, and her conversation was filled with such wisdom that others sought her advice.

In time, a husband was found for Chana. Chaim Leib Fleischman was able to look beyond her physical difficulties and see the wise, kind, helpful young woman she was. After their marriage in 1895, they had two daughters, and Chana was able to raise them into equally loving, dutiful women who respected and helped her even after they themselves were married.

Sarah, however, was of a totally different temperament. My grandfather wrote that, almost from the moment of her birth, she was able to charm and convince everyone else that she was too delicate to do the expected chores. She preferred wandering through the market with her friends, chatting, gossiping and watching any of the entertainers who traveled to Borchov to perform there. Lacking a photograph of Sarah to confirm my impression, I picture her as a pretty woman, with a strong, persuasive personality. Fortunately the young man, Archie Kowalek, who was betrothed to her, did not require her assistance in his business. He loved her dearly and was successful enough, especially after World War I, to provide her with a maid to help raise and care for their five children.

How different life was for Goldie, the youngest of the daughters. My grandfather wrote that as clever as Sarah was in avoiding work, so Goldie was willing to do whatever was asked of her and then offer her assistance to others in the household as she observed what else needed to be done.

Perhaps this was because she instinctively recognized that her birth was somewhat of a disappointment to her parents. After giving birth to three daughters, Faige Zeisel had hoped for another son. Their disappointment was cast aside when they realized that Goldie gave them more help than any of her older sisters.

She married Mendl Gross in 1897. Everyone in the family called him "Mendl Katzev," which means Mendl the butcher. The marriage appeared to be a good one. Mendl would boast and brag to everyone in Borchov that he was the richest butcher in town. And so he was. After he and Goldie had six children, he purchased a fairly good-sized house (by Borchov standards) and had it well furnished so that all could see how prosperous he was.

However, my grandfather described the difference between Archie Kowalek, Sarah's husband, who treated his wife with respect, generously giving her money to purchase clothes for herself and their five children, and Mendl Gross, who was very mean-spirited and miserly toward Goldie. He refused to allow Goldie to hire a maid to help her care for the children or the household, so she cooked, baked, scrubbed the house and sewed her own clothes as well as their children's. Mendl expected her to welcome frequent visitors to the house so that he could show off his success.

Eventually, all of this work took its toll and in her later years Goldie suffered from many aches and pains. Her only comforts were seeing five of her six children marry and then welcoming grandchildren into her life.

At the same time they were incurring debt to give dowries to their daughters, Faige Zeisel and Leib Yosef were increasingly disappointed and frustrated by their second son, Yeheskal. In addition to being a poor student who skipped away from his classes at the *cheder*, he was the subject of gossip because of the young girls with whom he began to flirt.

Faige Zeisel and Leib Yosef reluctantly concluded that Yeheskal was not suited for the life of a student. They were willing to support him if he was studying, but the times were too difficult to allow him to idle away his days. So they permitted him to leave the *cheder* and find a job helping someone who had a business in the market. He really wanted to be a farmer. Renting a small plot of land with enough room to grow vegetables or raise a few chickens would take a sizeable amount of money, which Yeheskal did not have. The meager wages Yeheskal earned working for someone did not even cover what he spent on amusements and in coffee houses.

In the informal setting of the coffee house, Yeheskal and his friends would gossip, tell stories, discuss the political situation in their country and in neighboring Russia and eventually come to debate the eternal question, "Where do we go from here?"

Following the assassination of Czar Alexander II of Russia, in 1881, Jews all over Eastern Europe, but especially in the

Pale of Settlement, were coming to realize that their only hope for survival was to leave. This push for emigration traveled over the border to Galicia.

Some of Yeheskal's friends might have suggested going to the cities of Europe, such as Lvov or Warsaw, where there were jobs in factories. Others would have pointed out that these jobs paid low wages and that conditions in the cities were crowded and unhealthy. The decisive argument for many was that they would still be living in an Eastern European country under laws that repressed the Jews.

There was a group of Zionists in Borchov that advocated leaving for Palestine, the place that was the ancient land of *Eretz Yisroel* where Jews had lived independently in their own country centuries before.

Others might have countered by pointing out that the coveted land was now under the rule of the Ottoman Empire, whose caliphs refused entry to the Jews. In addition, the land would have to be purchased from its current owners. How would they pay for this? A further argument was that after centuries of lying fallow, the land had reverted to being a desert and it would take a massive effort to make it bloom again.

Among the ultra-Orthodox, the whole concept of going back to the ancient homeland and creating a secular state was pointless and irrelevant. They believed that only when the Messiah returned could they again live there.

At this point, someone would always say, "We should go to America." The debate would be re-energized. America was the *goldene medina*, a land of opportunity where Jews, as well as people of all races and religions were welcome. "The streets are paved with gold," another would always report. A Jew could travel freely throughout the country without identity papers, become a citizen, vote, send his children to university to become a doctor, a lawyer, an engineer.

"Yes, but," someone else would ask, "can you live a Jewish life there? Are there synagogues? Can you buy kosher food? My cousin wrote that he has to work on *Sabbos*."

Yet another opinion would come from someone arguing that the best solution was to stay and join a local movement that sought to bring Jews into the national government. Jews were to be encouraged to join such political parties.

The debate would rage on and only weariness and the need for sleep caused it to stop, to be continued the following night.

Yeheskal probably listened to all these points of view and concluded that going to America was the correct choice for him. He began badgering his parents to allow him to leave Borchov for the *goldene medina*. Before he could depart, however, he had to earn money for the trip. Once he had adopted this goal, his whole lifestyle changed. He no longer frittered away his time on amusements or frivolous activities. He worked long hours and saved his money.

Seeing his determination, Faige Zeisel and Leib Yosef relented and gave Yeheskal permission to leave Borchov. He would be the first of the Leib Yosef Neuringer family to leave, but he would not be the first Borchover. Others had begun leaving in the latter part of the nineteenth century, joining a large wave of emigrants from all over Eastern Europe, both Jewish and non-Jewish.

In 1900, when Yeheskal was eighteen, he boarded a train that would take him to one of the ports on the Baltic Sea coast, where he would find a ship to take him across the Atlantic Ocean. Their goodbyes must have been emotional. Faige Zeisel and Leib Yosef did not know if they would ever see Yeheskal again, despite his promise to return for a visit. And he could not be sure that he would be able to keep that vow. For every family, each time someone left, it was a painful wrench.

Once in New York, Yeheskal was helped by those Borchovers who had arrived before him. That was the way of immigrants to the New World. Used to living in countries where governments were cruel to them at the worst or indifferent at best, Jews had traditionally created organizations to help themselves.

By 1897 enough Borchovers had come to New York to form the First Borchover Sick Benefit Society. In America, these organizations were usually based upon the shtetl or area where they had lived and were known as *Landsmanschaften*. According to the society's constitution, its aim was "to support sick and needy members and establish brotherly friendship and behavior amongst its members."

Knowing that this society existed was a small consolation for Faige Zeisel and Leib Yosef in letting Yeheskal leave.

Soon after Yeheskal and the other Borchovers, among them members of the Fahrer family, cleared the immigration procedures at Ellis Island and stepped onto the streets of New York City, they realized that the streets were not paved with gold. Rather, the Lower East Side, the area where the newly arrived lived, was crowded, noisy and dirty, and life was difficult. Yeheskal had been accustomed to hearing the babble of many languages in Borchov. Once in New York, he heard Italian, Chinese and English spoken with an Irish lilt, saw black people for the first time and experienced a different kind of discrimination. It was in this "New World" that he encountered derisive jokes made over his Galician roots. According to those who came from Lithuania and other northern European communities as well as the wealthier Jews of German background, Galicians were country bumpkins – uneducated, uncultured and ill-mannered.

Nevertheless, Yeheskal continued his hardworking, ambitious ways. He lived so frugally that the *landsmen* from Borchov with whom he lived teased him about being a miser. Yeheskal ignored their taunts. He began sending as much money as he could back to his parents.

It was an amazing turn; with Yeheskal's money, Faige Zeisel and Leib Yosef were able to pay off all the debts that had accumulated when they married off their four daughters and paid their dowries. By going to New York, Yeheskal became a greater help to his parents than he had been while living in Borchov.

While the three younger daughters, Chana, Sarah and Goldie, seemed to be settled in their marriages and were raising their own children, Aiga and Haskall continued to struggle.

By the time the nineteenth century ended, Faige Zeisel and Leib Yosef had married off their four daughters, incurring debts for their dowries. They had welcomed their sons-in-law into their growing extended family and rejoiced at the births of their grandchildren.

The new century began with one son, Yeheskal, leaving Borchov. It continued with the death of their beloved first-born son, Shlomo, in 1904. Nevertheless, Faige Zeisel and Leib Yosef were resilient; their faith remained strong; they would continue to live as they had before, meeting and overcoming obstacles with prayer and determination.

Chapter 9:

A Time of Anxiety

The promise of the new century bringing prosperity and new beginnings did not last. The economy of the small shtetls declined as the pull of the larger cities in Europe and North America grew ever stronger. At the same time there were portents of the political upheavals that were to come.

War broke out between Russia and Japan in 1904. An attempt to overthrow the Czar in Russia in 1905 was brutally extinguished. The Balkan states were restive, and small wars erupted in the area.

The difficult economic times created particular hardship for Aiga, Haskall and their five children. Although a willing, conscientious worker, Haskall could not find a job in Borchov that paid him enough to support his family. As many in Borchov and hundreds of thousands of people all over Europe were doing, Aiga and Haskall looked to America as the place where they would find economically secure conditions to raise a family.

Pregnant with her sixth child, Aiga encouraged Haskall to leave Borchov on his own, find work in America, send money back to her and then, when he was established, send funds for passage for Aiga and the children. Her younger brother, Yeheskal, was already living in New York, sending money back to Faige Zeisel and Leib Yosef. This was the plan.

Haskall began his long journey, first by train to one of the ports on the Baltic Sea coast and then by ship to New York. He found work in New York City and began sending money back to Aiga and the six children. This was not an unusual occurrence. Many husbands and fathers as well as single, unmarried men left the shtetls first, sending for their wives, children and parents later.

Around this time Yeheskal met a young girl named Becky who had emigrated with her parents from Romania. He asked her parents if they would permit him to marry her. His was the only marriage not arranged by his parents. After the wedding Yeheskal continued working, but he could no longer send money back to his parents in Borchov as he now had a wife to support. Soon their first child, a son whom they named Benny, was born.

Yeheskal's love of Borchov, the fields surrounding it, and his dream of becoming a farmer never ceased. He longed to have his parents meet his wife and son. He knew that he could only return when he had enough money to set up a business. Becky agreed that she and Benny would leave for Borchov and Yeheskal would follow a few months later with his savings. Eight months after Becky and Benny arrived in Borchov, Yeheskal joined them. He used the money he brought with him to begin buying and selling cattle.

As the years of the new century passed, the time had come for the youngest member of the Neuringer family to marry. As yet, we have not been able to discover when my Grandfather Levi married Clara Fahrer. Since my father, their eldest son, was born on 7 June 1909, it is reasonable to conclude that it could have taken place as late as mid-1908. It is also reasonable to assume that the marriage was arranged in the same way that my grandfather's sisters' and eldest brother's had been.

We also do not know what qualities in the prospective bride and groom had appealed to the other family. Since my grandfather's memoir ends abruptly, we do not know how he was making a living at the time of his marriage, nor do we know how Clara's father, Alter Fahrer, supported his family.

Clara and Levi named their first-born son (my father) Shlomo Itzhak after Levi's eldest brother, who had died in 1904. Nearly three years later, Clara gave birth to a second son, on 8 February 1912, and named him Yisroel.

The exclamations of *mazel tov* that were given at my uncle's *bris* were still echoing when the news from outside Borchov depressed everyone's mood. There was constant talk of war; all the countries of Europe seemed to be aligning themselves in support of one dominant country or another. In fact, one "small war" had broken out in the Balkans in October of that year, a precursor to World War I.

Talk of an expanded war was becoming louder and more frightening. Once again, Yesheskal was planning to travel to New York, this time leaving his wife, Becky, and two sons in Faige Zeisel and Leib Yosef's care; a second son, Shmuel, had been born in Borchov.

Once again, Yeheskal decided to leave Borchov for the economic opportunities to be found in New York. Once again, he would leave Becky behind, this time in Galicia with their two sons. As soon as he found a job and paid off his debts, he would send money for their passage to New York. He arrived in New York on 3 September 1912.

When Yeheskal left Borchov a second time, he had no idea how long it would be before he saw his beloved wife, Becky, and his two sons again.

Aiga's oldest children from her first marriage, Harry and Mindy, also traveled to New York at this time. They were going to join their stepfather, Haskall. Why was he was willing to take on the responsibility for them while their mother, Aiga, stayed behind in Borchov with his own three young children?

Yeheskal Neuringer

Given the circumstances, it was a wise and thoughtful decision that Aiga and Haskall made. They understood that if war broke out, Harry was old enough to be drafted and they were desperate to prevent this. In addition to the hardships and dangers of the soldier's life, a Jewish soldier was not able to fulfill the commandments of his Jewish religion. The Emperor's soldiers were not able to eat kosher food, celebrate

Shabbos or any of the other Jewish holidays. In fact, both the Czar of Russia and the Emperor of the Austro-Hungarian Empire used the draft to wean Jewish boys away from their religion.

Going to America would be Harry's escape from the clutches of the Austro-Hungarian army. In addition, he and Mindy were old enough to work once they arrived in New York. It would take less time to purchase tickets for Aiga and her three younger children if three people pooled their savings than if Haskall was working on his own.

As the first years of the new century passed, the Neuringer family expanded with the births of grandchildren, while other members of the family left for America.

Chapter 10:
A Troubled Marriage

It is not unusual for financial difficulties to cause strains in a marriage. We know from the letters Clara wrote in 1914 that she was running a store where she sold wheat and other grains. It is possible that my grandfather took over his mother's business, minus the baking.

What is clear from the 1914 letters, however, is that the business faced many financial challenges. On the one hand Clara owed money to her suppliers, and on the other hand she needed to collect money from those who purchased goods from her.

Yeheskal's and Haskall's families are two examples within the Neuringer family where families were separated when the husband and father left for America to seek his fortune, later sending for his wife and children. There are also stories of husbands and fathers leaving, abandoning their wives and children to a life of penury and grief in the "old country."

My grandparents' story does not fall into either of these categories. The letters tell us that Levi left Clara and his two young sons abruptly and in a fury. According to Leib Yosef's 24 March letter to Yeheskal in New York, it was Clara who chased Levi out of the house. Leib Yosef wrote that even after he pleaded with Levi to stay, at least until after Pesach. His son replied:

> Every day I'm being chased out of my father's house. What will you accomplish if you don't let me go? Then you'll cry even more. I can't stand it anymore. I have to leave. I have to get rid of this buzzing in my head.

Leib Yosef continued, "...he had to leave. We finally agreed. We wished him to depart in peace. He didn't even say good-bye to us properly."

This letter is compelling not only for its content. Within the same envelope, Leib Yosef had enclosed a letter to each of his sons. Surely, Leib Yosef knew that each of his sons would have been able to read both letters. To Yeheskal, he wrote the story of why Levi had to leave. To Levi, he described his and Faige Zeisel's reaction to their youngest son's departure. Leib Yosef set down his version of why Levi had left, and it clearly shows that Leib Yosef believed Clara was thoroughly to blame. He must have understood, as well, that Levi could tell his brother his own story, if it differed from his father's. It is also possible that Yeheskal received the letters and welcomed his brother's arrival at the same time.

Leib Yosef had the money to undertake the voyage at short notice, so it is likely that my grandfather was already planning to leave for New York to make money, as his brother Yeheskal had done two years before. Nevertheless the actual timing of his departure was clearly a result of marital discord.

Records at Ellis Island show Levi arriving in New York on the SS *Noordam* on 1 April 1914. He was 29 years old at the time. He joined Yeheskal, who was living there alone, having left his wife, Becky, and sons, Shmuel and Benny, back in Borchov in 1912. Yeheskal was planning to save enough money to send for them.

Did Levi intend to do the same? Leib Yosef wrote to Levi:

> I tell you that you took away half our lives. Whom do you leave us to depend on? You compared us to your father-in-law, whose two sons are already in America, but he has at least one good son-in-law, Shimon Miazlevitz. But we old folks: to whom will

we be able to turn? Only God, may he help us. May God help that you should have good luck, good fortune and come home soon. That would give us encouragement.

The 26 April letter includes a postscript from Faige Zeisel who wrote pleadingly:

I ask you, my dear son, please try to send me the 30 [coin; unclear] that your wife collected. With that you will keep me alive because things are so bad for me presently that I don't know what to do. I wouldn't bother you, but I have nowhere left where I can borrow, and no one wants to give me even a sack of flour on credit. So I ask you to immediately send it to my address, not to your wife because she has other places where she can get, and she won't give to me. So I ask you to send it directly to me. From your mother, Faige Zeisel.

From this, and from Leib Yosef's comments, it appears that my great-grandparents wanted my grandfather to return because they were relying on his financial support, not necessarily because they wanted the family to be reunited. Dutiful son that he was, Levi did send money to his parents. Among the receipts that my cousin Martin Neuringer found was one dated 26 October 1919. This shows that my grandfather sent thirty-five dollars to "Leib Josef Neuringer" via American Express. This would have been exchanged into 2000 Polish kroner.

Clara also expects her husband to return. The first communication we have from her is a postcard written on 30 April, where she addressed Levi as, "My dearly beloved husband." She explains that she previously wrote two letters to her brother's address, which he apparently didn't receive. This card was sent to Levi in care of a banker, Adolf Mandel, who had an office on Rivington Street on the Lower East Side.

In a long, rambling letter written a few days later on 5 May, Clara began:

> My esteemed husband, Levi,
> I received your awaited letter. I shed tears as I read of your difficult situation and the fact that you left two such sons behind.
> Secondly, it hurts me that we are separated, that you are there and I am here, and in addition I am with your dear mother. In brief I have to tell you that may God help us! May God help that we should overcome all our troubles and we should be reunited again with our two children.

Neither the earlier postcard nor this letter contains any reference by Clara to Levi's sudden departure. If she was aware of her role in his decision or had any regrets over her behavior, she might have written about it in the earlier letters that were sent to her brother's address. The only reference here to their relationship is that they should "overcome their troubles."

Clara also describes the effect her husband's departure had on both her and their sons:

> Ever since Pesach the child has been very sickly and he wants to be held all the time. And I had to carry on holding him in my arms while I filled some sacks with flour. My arms are breaking.
> You ask if I would have use of you at this time. Of course it's true. Naturally, it would be easier if there were two of us.
> You write letters that cause me aggravation. And to the "little ones"? You write that they should have pleasure? What are you thinking about? Why do you

do that? If you don't [have] *mazel*, you also don't have common sense. Don't you know that they can't read by themselves, and don't you understand that the letters that you write cause a greater impression on my health?"

She is obviously upset and angry here. This is the first reference on the effect his leaving had on her health.

Further on she commented:

And if you will, with God's help, come home, you'll cut out all this nonsense. Considering the situation, then we will be able to live a contented life. May it be so already! I assume you want the same ... I am writing to you like a faithful wife to my husband, and I write you all about the children. I look forward to the time when we should be able to rejoice together with our children...

Now you ask me about the oldest son at Pesach time. May he be well and have much luck. Amen!

Also, if he asked the Four Questions. I can write you that he knew them very well and said himself that "next year I should ask my father" and he told Yisroltzi to say Amen!

Interspersed between her description of her feelings of loneliness and her children's reaction to Levi's absence, Clara wrote of her financial difficulties.

Now, my husband, you want to know if I am accumulating debt? The creditors are coming and I'm going to give you a few examples. I have to have a big heart.

Sol and Yisroel as little boys

She then went on to detail some examples of both owing money to some people and trying to collect from others:

> In short, whoever I owe money to I am struggling to repay. But whoever owes me money is not paying attention.

She tells my grandfather there are some people who will only pay him directly. Earlier, Leib Yosef's letter of 24 March 1914, quoted Clara telling someone named Menashe, "Pay me what you owe me."

Leib Yosef wrote that Menashe replied,"I didn't take anything from you. I will send what I owe Levi to America."

Even Clara's sister Jides wrote to Levi. In her letter of 27 May, she described to her brother-in-law the difficulties Clara had with collecting some of her debts. Jides told Levi that Clara had been advised to take one of her debtors to court and assured him that Clara did not know she was writing to him.

Jides continued with a request that Levi advise her on the possibility of her son going to America. She concluded the letter by writing about someone, whose name was unclear:

> ...[he] sent 20K[kroner] for your dear children to Chaika's address so that she could buy the children clothes and shoes. So she collected it from the post, but she didn't buy the children anything. She used the 20K for goods. I cried at the fact that she didn't buy anything for the children with the 20K, but what can one do? I see how people are taking advantage of her, and she's not earning now. Things are tough now. She feels betrayed. I end my letter and I wish you good luck, and you should come home to your wife and children; that's to say, my sister.
>
> From me, sister-in-law,
> Jides Schneider

(She signed her name using the Roman alphabet.)

On 1 July, Clara wrote:

> ...I ask you very much, my dearest husband, to already forget what happened and think now only about coming back home. It's a shame every day that we are apart, especially our dear children. They wander about like lost sheep, and it's hard for me to see. I myself don't know what happened to them.

69

Nothing helps, even if I were to give them the whole store with all the money.

The young child still cries his heart out. It's hard for me to see this … Look what all this has come to, and the children long for their father. I hope that regardless God will help, and when times are better, we will be able to look back at it all from a better perspective.

In another letter whose date is unclear, Clara wrote:

…I think it would be better to suffer in Borchov less than in America with wife and children together … When you come home in good health, we will be able to talk face to face … In such a fashion we should be able to live out our years and bring up our children properly and not have any other worries.

Perhaps she had a premonition of what might lie ahead because on 13 July she wrote:

I don't know if you're doing like all the good men who leave home and then forget about back home.

All the while that Clara was struggling to both care for their children and keep the store going, she faced criticism and ridicule from her father-in-law and other members of the extended Neuringer family.

In his first letter to my grandfather on 24 March, Leib Yosef wrote:

Now I write about your wife. Just after you left, she immediately, that same day, in the morning, sent "Shayben" to see if the mother-in-law is still alive. But she was still in a good mood and *farpitzed*. But she started to cry because nobody comes into the store. People say that if Levi is not here, I shouldn't go in. Whoever sees her says that she is *meshuggah*. One minute she's singing and the next minute she is crying.

A month later, on 26 April, Leib Yosef once again wrote to his son Yeheskal in New York of the reasons Levi had to leave:

> I really hoped that he would leave after Pesach ... But since she drove him out of the house immediately after Purim, to her brother, the rich guy...

Further on, he described her reaction to a letter she received from Levi:

> ...she became so proud that she goes around with a swollen head. She says that he's changing toward her. "When he will come, he will know how to behave and will take care of the house rather than be gone all day. He will come so that I can feed him and he will know how to watch his spending...
>
> When somebody wishes that her husband should come home as soon as possible, she says to them, "Let him stay there. It's good for me here without him, better than with him. And if he will come home a few years later, he will know that I am a wife, so he will listen to everything that I say."
>
> The whole town is laughing because everyone knows very well that he left only because of her, not God forbid because of us, because we did everything possible that he shouldn't leave. But she was stubborn to spite, insisting that he should leave before Pesach.

Leib Yosef continues writing about the letter Levi wrote to

Clara and the fact that she showed it to someone named Leibl. After Leibl's "...conversation with her, he came and told us, 'I can't understand her at all. She's *meshuggah.*'"

According to Leib Yosef, it was to Leibl that my grandfather:

> ...told the whole truth ... He [Levi] told Leibl that he brought her some beer from the *Seudah* at Goldie's place [Goldie was my grandfather's sister], so she grabbed it and threw it in his face. And once he bought a piece of liver from Mendl [Goldie's husband]. She threw it in his face and bloodied his whole face. That's the kind of love between them.

After he completed his letter to Yeheskal, Leib Yosef wrote a short note to Levi:

> Now I'm writing to my dear son Levi. May you live long and be well.
>
> My dear son, I don't have much to write you because you don't write much to me either. I want you to know that your dear wife is well. She eats and drinks and looks lovely, and your dear children are also well. B'H. They come to me and your mother gives them *kreitzers* so they buy themselves bonbons and Chana gives them poppy seeds. And your wife is *farpitzed* every day, so I ask you not to have aggravation. Eat and drink and take care of yourself. Look well. Don't feel sorry that it cost you the few hundreds of all her *tzuris.* May God help you that you be well and successful. May you come home speedily to your dear wife and your dear brother together. Your wife had a suit made by Moshe Stoller and purchased everything, even the boots. Don't take it to heart because of the money because she had enough money to divide up for us in our old

72

age, and you made mother so sick in our old age. We send you regards. May you merit to see us in good health. Amen. Leib Yosef Neuringer

The tone of this letter appears to be at cross-purposes. On the one hand, he appeals to his son to return home for the sake of his children and parents. On the other hand, he is describing Clara's activities and expenditures in an unkindly, unflattering way. This certainly doesn't suggest that Levi would return home and recreate a peaceful, loving family!

Much is made of Clara going around town, *farpitzed* or taking money meant for the children to have a suit made for herself. We have to remember that in a small town such as Borchov, it was hard to keep family business private. Gossip and the women who gossiped were mainstays of shtetl life.

In the album of pictures my father took in 1933 when he visited Borchov, there is one of a group of women sitting on a bench outside a house. When my cousin, Rita Eisenband, saw this picture, she wrote to me that this was the infamous bench that was feared by all the women in town. The bench was situated in a fairly central location; all Borchov's *yentas* sat there people watching. Rita recounted how her mother, Faige Zeisel, told her that she had to dress especially carefully if she knew she would walk past that bench, with so many pairs of eyes looking at her, passing judgment on her attire.

If that was the case in the 1930s, surely other women of an earlier generation were tried in the same court of public opinion. Any woman wearing a new outfit would have been noticed, and its style and appropriateness appraised.

This custom traveled to New York. I remember passing the guardian ladies who sat on benches or their own folding chairs on the sidewalks in front of the apartment buildings in the

Brooklyn neighborhood where I grew up. They would usually assemble after lunch to sit, observe, comment and judge. My mother always made sure that she was properly dressed, seams on her stockings straightened, hair combed and lipstick on before going out, even to the corner grocery store. From my teenaged years on, I was cautioned to do the same, as "you never know who you might meet."

Three unidentifed women on the infamous bench

Clara was aware of the gossip, but was feisty, defending herself, describing arguments she had with her sister-in-law, Becky, Yeheskal's wife in a letter of 5 May.

> Becky "Klatzak" stirred things up by telling Jides what should I do ... She said that she can't stand my talk. This was all before Purim, after your departure ... The whole story is that they treat me so badly ... Woe, my most beautiful years are quickly running away. But I'm still hoping. In short I said to myself, "It's not what people say. God would not desert me and the young children."

She described how her mother-in-law, Faige Zeisel, "discouraged some *yentas* ... that [they] shouldn't buy from me... "

It appears that Levi was also corresponding with Becky, Yeheskal's wife, and Clara was angry about that.

> Briefly imagine my big tzuris. In addition to everything else, they are writing to you that I go around and *putz*. May God grant that this indeed be so, that I should go around happy and that I should be able to dress well.

After going on with more reporting of her financial situation and who owed her money, she mentioned that she had borrowed money from her sister, Jides, in order to enlarge the store.

> All of this is costing me a lot of money and energy. Pardon me many times over, my husband, for writing to you as though I were *musser* you. After all, you also write me in this vein, and I didn't get angry ... I'm already on page 20, and it's not even the beginning of what I had in mind to write. It's true that you always told me that I talk a lot, but what else can I do if people say that I talk a lot. I talk a lot because I know a lot. Therefore be patient with me now. Understand me and give me your earnest word.

One can question Clara's economic wisdom of borrowing money from Jides to enlarge the store at a time when she had so much debt. One month later, in her letter of 24 June, Clara wrote:

> I don't keep a girl anymore because I saw that it has to cost me a lot of money ... And Jides, as you

know, kept arguing with the girl. So I got rid of the
girl. It was hard, but now it's quiet.

Throughout her letters, Clara's words seemed to alternate
between defense of her actions and pleas for her husband's
return for the sake of the children. Her letters began with words
of endearment: "My dearly beloved husband," or "My
esteemed husband, Levi."

Were these genuine expressions of her feelings, or was
she following established social convention for florid
salutations? She described how the boys miss their father,
listed her perilous economic challenges, yet chided him for
previous behavior. Lacking any of the letters Levi wrote to
Clara, we have no way of knowing what he really wrote to
her at this time.

Except for the support from her beloved sister Jides she
does not appear to have had much sympathy from her in-laws
or friends.

Even more tzuris was shortly to befall Clara.

Chapter 11:
Breaking Point

If it weren't enough that Clara had to cope with her precarious economic situation, the alienation from her husband's family and the demands of raising two energetic little boys, one more disaster befell her.

Her mother, whose health had been failing, died. Alter Fahrer, Clara's father, actually sent a postcard to my grandfather in New York on 21 June, informing Levi that "the mother-in-law" died the week of 14 June, the week that *Parsha Shelach* was read.

> The time for her death had really come. She couldn't stand the pain in her whole body, especially in her legs. She prayed to God that he should have pity and take her soul (*nishama*).

As an aside, it is fascinating to observe that my great grandfather dated this note in Hebrew according to the Hebrew calendar *Yom Alef* (day one, i.e., Sunday) followed by the *Parsha* that was read that week: *Parsha Korach*.

The death of her mother had a profound effect on Clara's health.

On 24 June, she wrote to Levi:

> …my tzuris [troubles] started because of my faithful, beloved, God-fearing mother to whom I had to attend. That really brought me down completely. If you were to see me now, you wouldn't recognize me at all. That's how God treated me so I ask my dearly beloved husband to forget everything that happened,

and with God's help, pray for me and our dear sons, may they live.

After telling him that "...you are my only hope in the world," she continued:

> ...I have no more patience to write as I am very weakened from the tzuris, and it is now two weeks since I've been outside. Until a few days ago I couldn't go out. It was a bitter five days. May we be protected from such tzuris. Amen

Yet she goes on writing another four pages, much about the business that she described as:

> ...very weak. You can imagine, here I am sitting in the store, during the day, writing this letter from my deepest heart and with such pain. Only God can help me. And you, my eternally beloved husband, you may think that I'm exaggerating [?]. I write you that I hope that we will see each other as soon as possible in health and good fortune. We should be content with our lovely and precious two sons. May they be well and grow with *mazel*. I'm speaking the truth because my suffering now is very great to such an extent that I'm incapable of writing it all. I can't write you anymore because the tears are running from my head to my feet because of loneliness.

After telling him how much help her sister, Jides, has been to her, she closed the letter, but before she was able to mail it, she received one from Levi, and her mood immediately brightened:

> You can't imagine the joy that I had when I saw the letter ... I am incapable of writing you the joy the children had when I told them that there's a letter

from their father. But our Tzrultzi rejoiced and called out that I should give him paper to write a letter to father. People who come into the store ask him what he will write to his father. So he says he will ask father to send him a suit. So they tell him, "No. Write him that he should come home."

He started to write, "Father, come home."

Clara then responded to some of the questions Levi must have posed in his letter:

I really don't know what to answer about two matters: about the debts. It's true about what you write me. I have to have patience. Maybe with time I will gradually collect, and the second thing about the picture. That's also true. We really look bad but now I even look worse. May God grant that I should return to my former self as soon as possible. I am very grateful that you write me that you are well, thank God, and that you are already earning $8 a week. Nevertheless I can imagine your struggle and I hope that you won't suffer long. Kisses once more. Please answer promptly. Your Clara.

On 13 July 1914 she wrote:

Believe me, my dear Levenyu, I am so changed now, a transformation. I pray to God that as long as I will live I shouldn't have such tzuris and that all misfortune should avoid us in the coming year and that things should return for the better as soon as possible and that you should return home as soon as possible to your wife and children because our suffering is indescribable...

I can't write you in full because it would cause you anxiety. I myself can hardly bear it all. The situation has made me ill. It's more than two weeks that I'm very sick. You would have a shock if you saw what I look like ... Because of mother's death it has become very quiet in the house as though ten people would be missing...

She continued with a description of how her sister Jides was helping her, that her father was saying *kaddish* and that she hoped her brother Shimon would continue saying *kaddish* after the *Shloshim.*

Meanwhile it's very lonely for me ... I have to figure out what's going to be with me. I do a lot of crying and I don't have much appetite to eat and I do not sleep through the night and the children also do not sleep. I don't know what to do. I'm sick and my stomach also is not functioning well. I got meat from our brother-in-law Mendl. You can imagine that it's not good for me and I've lost all appetite because of it. Maybe God will help me finally so that I'll feel better. And may I get good letters from you.

At the end of the month, Clara finally went to a doctor. In a postcard written on 30 July, she wrote first on the back of the card:

My dear, sincere husband Levi,
I received your dear letter of encouragement today but I am a little weak to write you a comprehensive letter in reply. Since my dear mother departed from me such as never happened to me that I became sick from it myself. May you hear of my good health. To sum up, I was at the doctor's on Sunday because I've been suffering so much. He told me I'm very weak, and he gave me medicine to make me stronger, and he told me to take [unclear] baths and repeat 12 or 15 times. It costs [unclear] for

a package. Each container is for one bath. Every day I have to take a fresh bath. But I figure that I should be able to take at least 6 baths because it's very costly, and it's very hard for me. May God help me because I am very alone now. Beyond that, nothing.

On the front of the card Clara wrote:

I've lost all my appetite and I can't sleep, and I hope that with the baths I'll feel better. So I'm going to look into the baths. May God grant that in the next letter I'll have better news to write to you, both about myself and our dear children. Amen. Thank God they are well, but they look bad because children need parents. So warm greetings. Your lonely Clara. From deepest heart.

She also wrote something around the edge of the card, which is unclear and could not be read.

In her next letter, dated 3 August she told Levi, "Now I can write you about the baths. They made me very weak. The little child; may he be well, he tires me out. I have to be stronger than iron to endure it all."

After writing that her sister Jides was also going through difficult times, she repeated her comment about the baths: "But now I don't have any patience to write because I just had a bath, and I'm very weak from the bath."

We do not know what was in the packets that the doctor prescribed for Clara to put in her baths. It might have been something as simple as Epsom salts. Perhaps it was not the curative property of the powder that was so important. What was being prescribed was for Clara to have the opportunity to relax for an extended period of time in a hot, soothing bath, something we who have indoor plumbing in our homes take for granted. Clara was clearly depressed and anxious at this time.

There was a method of treatment used in the eighteenth and nineteenth centuries for "hysterical" women to be immersed in baths for long periods of time to calm them down. Perhaps what Clara's doctor prescribed was derived from that type of treatment.

Clara's physical concerns would only be compounded by the political upheaval that was about to take place in Europe. In August 1914, war broke out in Europe; World War I began.

Chapter 12:
World War I

Nachman Blumenthal, born in Borchov in 1905, edited and wrote much of *The Book of Borszczow* [the Yizkor Book]. I have to thank him for much of the content of this chapter. He began his chapter on World War I by describing what terrible anxiety there was throughout the Jewish community in Borchov, as well as in the rest of Eastern Galicia, when war in the Balkans erupted.

People there feared and mistrusted Russia, the vast country to the east. Generals of the Austro-Hungarian army were also worried about a Russian invasion and sent a company of soldiers to the shtetl. These soldiers were housed in one of the synagogues. Twice a day, early in the morning and later in the evening, Blumenthal and his friends watched the soldiers march, parade and perform their drills right in the street.

Their leader, the *hauptman*, rode a horse, accompanied by two hussars who wore red hats and blue coats. Fascinated by this military display, Blumenthal would sometimes follow the men as they marched right out of the village to a field where they practiced shooting.

Four soldiers with guns were stationed on the roof of the *gymnasium*. Blumenthal and his friends concluded that they were stationed there in case a Russian plane flew over Borchov. They expected the soldiers would shoot down the plane.

No one in Borchov had seen a real plane before. Once, during a patriotic demonstration that lasted until darkness fell, people thought they saw "the plane." It was high in the sky, and from the distance, Blumenthal thought it looked just like a star. Some people insisted that the object was observing everything that was happening in the streets below. Hours later the "plane" disappeared.

While for children such as Blumenthal this was a period of diversion, to watch and pretend what it would be like to be a soldier, for the teenaged boys and the adults this was a time of continued uncertainty.

On 28 June 1914, Archduke Franz Ferdinand, nephew of Emperor Franz Joseph I and heir to the throne, was assassinated in Sarajevo, Serbia. This was the match that lit the fires of the war that was to have ended all wars. War was declared on 4 August. On one side were Germany and the Austro-Hungarian Empire. On the other side were the armies of Czarist Russia, France, Great Britain (including troops from the Dominion of Canada), Italy and, after April 1917, the United States.

One immediate effect of this was that Aiga's plan to leave Borchov with her young children was blocked. Her sister-in-law, Becky, and her two sons Shmuel and Benny were trapped as well. There was no hope of their being able to take a train to the Baltic Sea coast and then a ship to America. To add to their misery, international postal service was also interrupted, so they could no longer receive any money from their husbands.

It meant that Levi, who had arrived in New York on 1 April 1914, also could not send any money back to his family in Borchov to help Clara care for their two sons – nor could he return.

Life in Borchov went on as usual until one Friday evening in August 1914. Blumenthal's father was on his way home from work when he heard an official shout: "General mobilization!" He repeated these two words to everyone he met, Jews and non-Jews.

Although Blumenthal didn't understand what the words meant, he noticed how everyone became immediately depressed. Women started to cry; they wailed that their husbands and sons must hide.

The next morning, *Shabbos*, the first train passed through Borchov, overflowing with those men who had been called up to serve in the army. A large group of women, children and older men stood on the station platform. Blumenthal observed that their faces were angry and streaked with tears, and their cries grew bitter. Blumenthal couldn't understand why they were crying. His idea of war was a fantasy – marching soldiers in handsome uniforms. He had no idea what being in a war was really like.

In her four-page letter of 3 August 1914, Clara wrote:

> Levenyu, if you could see Goldie's Yankel as a soldier and other such young fellows, you would laugh from tzuris. They all stand [stay] in Borchov because of *protectzia*. They got permission to go home every day.

At the end of the letter, she wrote:

> May God help us first to be well and the war end. Then I'll write you more. In America people probably know more about the war. Write me everything. Your eternal Clara.

In her last postcard from 1914, dated 11 August, she wrote about how anxious she was to receive a "good letter" from Levi.

That would really do me good because I'm now going around very troubled because I can't even earn a *kreitzer* for shopping. I have to take everything on credit.

A few days later a regiment of infantry marched through Borchov on the road toward Skala, a neighboring shtetl. The soldiers looked tired and disheveled. Some marched in groups, others trudged alone. Blumenthal joined the crowd watching them and found it difficult to believe that "his" army was marching in such a poor condition. Jewish people, perhaps Clara as well, stood on the sidewalks with jugs of water and tin cups, giving the soldiers drinks or distributing bread and rolls. The crowd wasn't very happy to see that the soldiers acted like beggars when they took these provisions.

Clara and the other Borchovers heard that after a few days in Skala, the regiment went over the Russian border. News came back that a Jewish officer had distinguished himself there. He fell during the battle, but before he died, he killed a Russian soldier.

The appearance of the regiment was much worse when they came marching back. Trains filled with provisions arrived after the army did, followed by ordinary wagons, driven by peasants because the army was short of military wagons. No one in Borchov understood it then, but the Austro-Hungarian army was poorly equipped, and the Empire would disappear by the end of the war.

Once more Borchov was quiet. A short time later, when the local *gendarme* officer rode into town, the letter carrier gave him a dispatch. That night the officer, together with the rest of the gendarmerie, disappeared. The mayor left as well. Borchov was left without anyone in control.

Everyone was very anxious. The shtetl was without a leader. If the Russians came, with whom would they speak? Who would defend the people of Borchov? Some Jews went to an old, former leader and begged him to take control of the village. He was Ukrainian and would, therefore, be able to speak to the Russians. They also thought that he had friendly relations with the Jewish community. Nevertheless they watched over him day and night to make sure that he, too, did not leave.

Several Jews hired some coachmen and wagons, loaded them with their wives, children and a few belongings and went to a shtetl that was a mile or two from Borchov. They believed that since this village was not on the main road, the Russian Army would not go there. Because of her physical condition it was impossible for Chana, Faige Zeisel and Leib Yosef's second daughter, to walk the distance to the neighboring shtetl. She stayed behind. Most of the family of Faige Zeisel and Leib Yosef also had no choice but to remain in Borchov.

Because there was no mail to or from New York, our knowledge of the war years comes from Nachman Blumenthal's account in the Yizkor Book.

The new mayor's first order was to have everyone hang out white flags, a sign that Borchov had surrendered, so that the Russians would not do anything to the people.

The Russians arrived the next afternoon. Blumenthal described the scene. First, one Cossack holding a rifle galloped in on a small horse. Then a second Cossack came, followed by a third. Blumenthal later described them as passing "like an arrow from a bow through the city."

Later one of the Cossacks galloped back. He stopped his horse in front of an inn and started to yell, "Vodka!" Lipster, the proprietor, came out of the house with a bottle of whisky and a small glass. After he filled the glass and gave it to the Cossack, the Cossack told Lipster to drink it himself, wanting to make sure that the liquid wasn't poison. Lipster drank the whisky and began to pour a second glass. The Cossack grabbed the bottle out of his hand and galloped off, holding it along with his horse's reins.

Shortly after, a giant mass of Russian Army men rode into town, led by a general. Seeing a few Jews in the market, he stopped and gave a short speech in Russian. Although the people didn't understand everything, they inferred that he and the army had come to free them from Austrian rule and not to fear, the Cossacks wouldn't do anything to harm them.

The general rode off, followed by an army that stretched a long way behind. Blumenthal stood on the sidewalk with his family and neighbors. He looked carefully at the Cossacks because he had heard a rumor that the Russians sent Tartars from the Caucasus to the front. These Tartars, so the story went, had only one eye in the middle of their foreheads.

Among the army personnel were doctors and medics with red crosses on their arms. Some of the Borchovers noticed a few Jewish faces among the army personnel. When the riders stopped for a while, people began to ask them if there were any Jews among them, Jews from the other side.

The Russians were in Borchov for three years. The soldiers were billeted in people's houses, the Tartars housed mainly by Jews. In this way, Blumenthal and his family were able to observe some of the Russian soldiers closely.

We do not know if any soldiers were housed with Clara or any other Neuringers, nor do we know if Clara was able to maintain her business.

Blumenthal noticed how very young some of these men were, a few not much older than he was. Their uniforms were ragged, their equipment old. As he listened to them speak to one another, he learned to speak a few words in Russian. As the months passed Blumenthal also observed that few of the soldiers could read or write. He could read the Hebrew in the prayer book as well as Yiddish and had just begun to learn to read and write German in the local *gymnasium* when the war broke out. Hebrew and Yiddish were written in the same alphabet, German a different one. Russian, Blumenthal noticed, was written in yet another alphabet, Cyrillic.

As time went on, the Russian soldiers could occasionally be seen helping the members of a Jewish family. One soldier actually rocked a Jewish child, someone noticed. Another helped in a Jewish store. A third one groomed a Jewish horse; a fourth one chopped wood for the Jewish housewife in whose house he lived.

Some Jews opened an inn where the Russian soldiers could come to drink tea and eat fresh buns. They paid the full price with rubles, the Russian currency. This was a change from the currency used before the war, the money of the Austro-Hungarian Empire. By doing business with the Russian soldiers, some of the Jewish Borchovers were able to make a good living.

The population of Borchov actually grew at this time, and not just from the Russian soldiers. One group of newcomers was composed of those who were forced out of nearby shtetls, including Skala, and they settled in Borchov. Other shtetls, such as those close to the Dniester River, were destroyed because of the fighting, and there was nowhere to house these people, so they, too, came to Borchov. They were particularly poor and in need of assistance. Blumenthal knew of other Jewish families who had also come from surrounding villages to Borchov, where they thought they would be safer.

Representatives from the Association of the Russian Cities came to Borchov and brought help to the people, especially the refugees. They established an aid association and opened a soup kitchen where they distributed meals and gave money to those in need. The representatives of this association that came to Borchov from Kiev were Jews: Shmuel Gomelsky and later Itzhak Gutterman.

In addition, two Russian military doctors, Dr. Bloch and Dr. Landau, both Jews, secretly helped the impoverished Jewish people. Since they were stationed in the military hospital in Borchov, they could help Jews in their free time. When they went on leave to Kiev or another large city, they used their own money to buy materials that people needed and then distributed them clandestinely. They also would ride to isolated shtetls in order to leave a few rubles for poor families.

Among the pictures in the album my father took on his visit back to Borchov in 1933, I found some that had been taken at an earlier time. One, undated with no caption on the back, is of a group of children. The little boy in the center is my Uncle Irv (Yisroel). Next to him is a girl and next to her is a boy whose face is out of focus. Therefore, I cannot tell if this is my father. The boys are each holding bowls, suggesting that this might be a soup kitchen or perhaps a school lunchroom.

The children are not smiling. Indeed, their faces are expressionless. Told to pose for a picture, they followed the instruction with no added emotion, giving no more than what was required. As I look at the picture, sitting as they are, wearing coats and hats in a room devoid of any adornment, I want to caption the scene, "Please, sir, may I have some more."

"Soup kitchen"

Some of the refugees remained in Borchov when the war ended. Blumenthal gained new friends whose families stayed because there was nothing for them to return to in their old villages.

After a while, Blumenthal forgot where his new friends were born. But his parents could tell from their last names that they weren't originally from Borchov. The tie between the Russian Jews and the Borchov Jews became strong. The people of Borchov became more aware of Jewish life beyond their own borders. Blumenthal began to hear stories of Jews belonging to political and revolutionary groups in Russia.

In spite of these few good relationships with the Russian soldiers, the Jews of Borchov still looked for their own soldiers to return safely. One of the Borchov "boys" who was drafted into the army was Shmuel Neuringer, my grandfather's nephew, who was my grandfather's deceased brother Shlomo's eldest son. Without parents to shelter him or possibly bribe officials, there was nothing Shmuel could do when the Austro-Hungarian officials seized a group of young Borchovers at the outbreak of the war.

When a Borchover heard any bit of news, he would eagerly pass this around to everyone else. Most Borchovers were genuinely sad when they learned that Emperor Franz Joseph I had died in November 1916. When they compared his treatment of Jews to the Czar's virulent hostility toward his Jewish subjects, they felt that they had been marginally better off.

Blumenthal and the others in Borchov were distressed to see the poor condition of Austrian and German prisoners of war when they were moved through the town on their way to prisoner-of-war camps. People would gather money, cigarettes and clothing for the prisoners and secretly pass the items to them, although the Russian authorities forbade this kind of contact. As they handed over the materials, the Borchovers would ask the prisoners where the front was, where they had been captured.

Some prisoners were willing to share information, especially after receiving the goods given to them. People were amazed to hear some prisoners say they were happy to have been captured. A few even made nasty remarks about the Austro-Hungarian and German armies and the leadership.

Life in Borchov continued to get more and more difficult for the people there. In addition to living in crowded conditions because of the refugees, the Jewish men – just Jewish men – grew afraid of being grabbed off the street by the Russians, to be used for unpaid labor. Some were put to work in the city smashing stones; others were marched off to nearby villages to dig trenches.

The Jewish community panicked even more when the Russians started grabbing girls for work. The girls were taken to a work camp outside Borchov. When the Russian commander of the camp showed up in the shtetl, people sent warnings through the village, and young girls raced into hiding. Aiga must have been particularly frantic each time this happened as she had three daughters, Rifke, Ruchel and Liba, to protect.

We have no information about how Clara was able to survive during those difficult years. If her business was precarious and burdened with debt before the war, it must surely have been even more difficult during this time. Also, given her depressed mental condition at the outbreak of the war, it is difficult to imagine her coping with the uncertainty of daily living. Whatever the circumstances we do know how deeply she loved her sons. She would have done everything possible to ensure that they were fed and secure.

A second disaster befell Borchov. Cholera broke out once again. Russian soldiers first caught the disease and it then spread among the rest of the population. Without proper medical attention and medication, very few sick people survived. My grandfather's sister Chana was one of those who became ill at this time. Her body, weak and frail since childhood, succumbed in 1916 to an illness that might have been cholera. She was 44 years old.

Once again, Faige Zeisel and Leib Yosef sat *shiva* for a child. This time, however, because of the epidemic, it appeared that every household was in mourning.

Blumenthal observed the wagons rolling through Borchov a few times each day, loaded with wooden stretchers that carried those who had died. A soldier wearing a white apron walked beside the wagon. He held the reins of the horse in one hand, and in the other was a whip. Under his arm was a flask of carbolic acid, which was used as a disinfectant.

When the non-Jewish cemetery filled up, the Russians commandeered a field opposite the Jewish cemetery and started to bury their dead there. Soon the local Christian people began to use it as well, and so Borchov gained a new gentile burying ground.

Some of the older Jewish people in Borchov remembered a way to rid the shtetl of this epidemic: the *kehilla*, or Jewish council, organized a wedding ceremony that was to be held in the Jewish cemetery. The people believed that holding a happy celebration such as a wedding in the cemetery would drive away tragic things from happening in future.

The bride was a poor girl, the gravedigger's daughter. The gravedigger could not afford a dowry for his daughter. The organizers chose a refugee, a young man with a limp, who wasn't considered a "good match" for any of the Borchov girls, to be the groom. Despite the heat of a summer day, the couple was dressed in typical wedding finery supplied by the villagers. The *callah* had a white veil covering her hair, and the *chusen* wore a fine frock coat.

Even the *klezmer* band was there to play appropriate wedding music as the groom came into the cemetery grounds. After the wedding, Blumenthal joined the crowd in accompanying the newly married couple to their new home. The *kehilla* had rented a room for them in someone's house.

Blumenthal recalled that the epidemic didn't stop immediately after the wedding, but everyone agreed that they felt their hearts lighten on that day. We have no record if any members of the Neuringer family attended the wedding in the cemetery. If my father and uncle were there, it would have been a carefree moment for them, diverting their attention from a precarious existence.

Blumenthal was beginning to understand why people wept at the outbreak of the war. He no longer saw it as a romantic event. Some of his friends died in the plague, and the meals his mother prepared barely filled his growling stomach.

Shlomo Seinfeld Rappoport, a social activist, journalist and writer who used the pen name Ansky, wrote another description of Borchov at this time. He is most famous for his play, *The Dybbuk*. During the years of the Russian occupation he traveled from shtetl to shtetl gathering folk material and lived in Chortkiev, near Borchov, for a while.

Blumenthal wrote that after the war Ansky published *The Destruction of Galicia*. One of the references to Borchov in the book describes the trials of eleven people who were probably charged with spying for Austria, convicted and hanged.

Another section in Ansky's book describes how 1,500 people, originally from Skala, moved to Borchov in 1916 because the Russian authorities did not let them return to their destroyed city.

A third passage tells how the Ziemski Association opened an orphanage for approximately 100 Jewish children. Women from the community volunteered to care for them. They spoke Yiddish to the children and taught them songs and games. The orphans were housed in a building that was owned by a Ukrainian who lived upstairs from the facility.

Back in New York, Yeheskal, Levi and Haskall read the news printed each day in the Yiddish paper, the *Jewish Daily*

Forward. Partly they hoped that the United States would enter the war so that it would finally end. They were aware that the Austro-Hungarian Empire was crumbling. They did not want their families to be left under Russian rule. They prayed that their parents, wives and children would be safe. There was not much more that they could do.

In 1917, another upheaval occurred that would bring massive changes to Borchov: in Russia, revolution had erupted. The monarchy was overthrown; the Czar and his family were arrested and imprisoned.

Chapter 13:

After the Russian Revolution

Ever since he could remember, Nachman Blumenthal had heard stories about how cruel the Russian Czar was, not only to the Jews who lived in that country, but also to his own people. He knew that the Czar's government had decreed that the Jews could not live in the large cities, such as Moscow, that were beyond the Pale of Settlement. They needed special permission if they wished to travel outside the Pale for business purposes.

In 1905, communists, socialists, anarchists and other groups in Russia rose up, attempting to force the Czar into granting reforms to the repressive government. The Czar responded by ordering his troops to shoot the protesters. In 1917, the people revolted again, and this time they succeeded in overthrowing the Czar.

After the Russian Revolution, Dr. Landau, the Jewish doctor in the Czar's army who had first come to Borchov with the invading Russian troops, returned to the shtetl as an official representative of the newly formed Russian power. Borchovers remembered him because of the assistance he had secretly given to needy people during the years of Russian occupation.

Blumenthal went to the synagogue with the other men to hear Dr. Landau's speech, which lasted for several hours late into the night. He spoke about the revolution and suggested that Borchovers elect a "national committee" for the town. Blumenthal could sense the mood of the men changing as they listened to the Russian doctor. They all knew that Dr. Landau was a *mensch* and believed him when he affirmed that the new

Russian government would not be anti-Semitic, that Jews would have equal rights. From then on, Borchovers followed the events happening in Russia with great interest.

The first result of the revolution was that the Czarist Russian Army withdrew from fighting in the war; their troops left Borchov and the other shtetls and cities in Galicia. Before they left, however, many retreating soldiers robbed the people, and there was fear of pogroms.

It was with relief and happiness, then, that the people welcomed the return of the Austro-Hungarian soldiers who lived in the local area. For the first few days, there was general rejoicing in the shtetl.

One of those soldiers who returned was Shmuel Neuringer, Shlomo's oldest surviving son. He had been wounded while fighting, and it took him many years to recover completely. His two younger brothers thanked God that what remained of their family was together again. Nevertheless, both Mattityahu and Herman began making plans to join their Uncle Yeheskal in New York as soon as it became possible for them to travel.

Borchovers were mistaken if they thought that life would return to the way it had been before the war. There were two more years of upheavals to live through. People began to notice that some of the soldiers who were returning were now members of the German army. They were displaying ominous signs of anti-Semitism and began forcing Borchover boys into their army.

Both the German and the Austro-Hungarian armies were getting weaker. The Austro-Hungarian Empire finally surrendered to the Allies on 4 November 1918, a week before the German Army did, and the Ukrainians took over governing western Galicia and Borchov. A Ukrainian

Democratic Republic was established, and Jews were promised the same rights as everyone else. A central Jewish National Committee was established with headquarters in Lvov and later in Stanisloi.

Borchovers had high expectations for this group. Among other things, they hoped for the establishment of Jewish schools and that Yiddish would be recognized as the official language.

However, the Polish Army kept up pressure on the poorly equipped Ukrainians, and the territory that they administered kept getting smaller and smaller. The new government finally moved its capital to a nearby town, Chortkiev. They couldn't even hold on to that for long. A short time later, the Ukrainian Democratic Republic moved its headquarters to the east, and with that, the hopes of Borchov being included in the new Republic disappeared.

Once more the shtetl was left without anyone in power. Borchovers were very afraid of the Poles whose arrival was imminent.

In November 1918, rumors went flying through the marketplace that the Poles had led a pogrom in Lvov. Blumenthal heard that the Poles had taken Jews walking on the street, cut off their beards and *payes* and beaten the men up. The community organized a gathering in the synagogue to mourn those who had been killed.

Shortly after, the Polish Army did arrive in Borchov. They did not initiate any pogroms against the Jews, but the Poles conscripted Jews – only Jews – for forced labor, just as the Russians had done earlier. They even apprehended Jews on *Shabbos* when men were returning from attending services in the synagogue. Those who had been taken were put to work cleaning the stables and sweeping the barns where the Polish soldiers kept their horses. The worry that they too might be taken must have made Mattityahu and Herman even more anxious to leave for New York.

At the same time, the Poles began to persecute those who had supported the Ukrainian Democratic government. Whether they had or had not sympathized with the Ukrainians, the accusation "Jew Bolshevik" was hurled at them. Jews and non-Jews who worked for the Ukrainian Democratic government were fired from their jobs.

There was yet another upheaval when the Bolsheviks (revolutionaries) from Russia took over the village again. A revolutionary committee of five people was established, including two Jews. However, this regime did not last long either.

At the Peace Conference in Paris in 1919 the Austro-Hungarian Empire was officially divided into separate countries. Western Galicia, including Borchov, was given back to Poland, which had governed the land so long ago. The Poles returned and controlled Borchov until the outbreak of World War II.

Once again, Borchovers had to learn a different language in order to conduct official business with the new government. Few Jews spoke Polish. In many cases, the children, who were now able to attend public school and the *gymnasium*, brought the Polish language into the home.

It was during this time of political turmoil and uncertainty – the fall of 1920 – that Leib Yosef died. After chanting *Kol Nidre*, one of the most solemn prayers in the Jewish prayer book, on Yom Kippur eve, Leib Yosef collapsed. Faige Zeisel and their three daughters Aiga, Goldie and Sarah, were with him.

It is an Orthodox Jewish tradition for a man to sit with a dead body, chanting prayers until the funeral, which ordinarily takes place within twenty-four hours of the death. Since Leib Yosef's two surviving sons, Yeheskal and Levi, were living in New York, his former students took turns in watching over his body and saying the memorial prayers.

Leib Yosef was 77 years old at his death. He had seen many changes in his lifetime, mourned the death of his eldest son, a daughter and grandchildren, and lived through the destruction and upheaval of war. Yet he lived to see all of his children marry and to celebrate the births of many grandchildren. When he was born, he had lived in the Austro-Hungarian Empire. Upon his death, his shtetl, Borchov, was now in Poland, as it had been hundreds of years before.

Leib Yosef's beloved wife, Faige Zeisel, who had been his helpmate for most of his life, lived a scant nine months more before she too died. She was 75 years old.

Chapter 14:

Reunions and Separations

The end of World War I also meant that those whose plans to leave had been interrupted by the hostilities could now begin their journeys. Borchovers hastened to larger towns and cities or left Europe altogether for North or South America, Australia, Palestine or whichever country would grant them entrance.

There was a rising tide of urgency to this emigration because, like a river is dammed to prevent it from overflowing, so were the borders of countries where people wanted to go beginning to be closed to slow the rush of immigrants.

In 1921, the United States Congress passed the Emergency Quota Act, the main purpose of which was to limit immigration from Eastern Europe and Italy. Under the quota for each country, preference was given to unmarried people under the age of 21 and to children and spouses over the age of 21.

Under these provisions, many families that had been divided could now be reunited. In 1923, Aiga left Borchov with her three youngest children, Ruchel, Liba and Gershon, and was reunited in New York City with her husband, Haskell, and children Mindel and Harry. Her eldest daughter, Rifke, however, remained in Borchov.

By this time, Rifke was married and had children, one of whom was a daughter that she had named after her beloved grandmother, Faige Zeisel. According to Rifke's granddaughter, Rita, the family was unable to emigrate to the United States because Lazar, Rifke's husband, had eye infections and therefore was unable to pass the health requirements. Only the fit were welcome to enter the United States. Therefore, for the rest of her life, until the outbreak of World War II once again interrupted the flow of mail and the transfer of money, Aiga again sent money to sustain Rifke and her family.

Becky, Yeheskal's wife, was finally able to leave Borchov with her two sons. She left behind some debts she had acquired because she had to borrow money from friends and relatives in order to feed her children. As soon as he could, Yeheskal paid off these debts. Yeheskal had given up his dream of being a farmer in Borchov, and he had a good job in New York City. After he greeted Becky and his sons at the ship's dock, he proudly took his family home to the house in Brooklyn he had been able to buy with the money he had saved. The house had a small backyard where he could grow flowers and some vegetables. In 1922, within a year of their reunion, Becky and Yeheskal had a third son, named him Joseph, and never again traveled back to Borchov.

Sadly, Ycheskal, who was now called Charlie, did not live a long life. He died of a stroke in 1931, when his youngest son was only nine years old.

Shlomo and Batya's two youngest sons Mattityahu and Herman also joined the stream of emigrants traveling to New York where they were united with their uncles Yeheskal and Levi. Perhaps they fit into the quota from Poland that, in 1924, allowed 5,982 people to enter the United States. Their older brother, Shmuel, remained in Borchov, still recovering from the wounds he had received while in the army.

One family not reunited after the war ended was my own. My Grandfather Levi did not send for my Grandmother Clara – only their two sons, my father and uncle.

Why not? This remains one of the biggest mysteries of the family saga.

Since my grandfather's memoir ends so abruptly we do not have his account of the events of the time. I can, however, speculate on some possibilities of what may have happened.

It is possible that although Levi was prepared to seek a better life in New York, Clara was not interested in leaving her father and extended family. We created this myth, convincing ourselves that this explained why she remained in Borchov.

A more reasonable possibility is that in spite of Clara's entreaties of "...when are you coming back?", Grandfather Levi never intended to return.

Although my grandfather did wire money to Clara while my father and uncle were still in Borchov, and he sent for them to join him in New York, perhaps his marriage was never a happy one. Certainly the derogatory, mocking comments Leib Yosef made about Clara's behavior after Levi left would only underscore any negative feelings that my grandfather already had about her.

After reading the letters, I believe that he had already intended to leave and did so sooner than planned because of Clara's outburst. This would explain how he had the funds to begin his journey on such short notice.

A third explanation for her not emigrating, however, could focus on my grandmother's mental condition. By her own admission and description, her mental state after her mother's death was troubled. Leib Yosef describes symptoms of erratic behavior in his letters to both Levi and Yeheskal in New York. He calls her *meshuggah*.

At this point we have to ask what Leib Yosef meant when he called Clara *meshuggah*. The term, meaning crazy, is often used as a pejorative but does not necessarily imply that the person is suffering from a mental disorder. The frequent connotation is that the *meshugganah* is silly, ridiculous, stupid or *fahrmished* [mixed up].

There is no doubt that her last letters of August 1914 show a deeply troubled woman whose anguish led her to seek medical advice. Did she have periods of such depression before Levi departed for New York? There is a suggestion that this was so in a letter she wrote around 14 July:

> As I write I don't know myself what I'm doing or what I'm saying, but I have to write and unload my heart. I feel that when I write you a letter, I feel better. When Monday arrives, that's the worst. I can't even write you how bad it is. Now it's already the fourth Monday since my dear mother died and we've already erected a stone, so you can imagine my sorrowful tone. Yes, my husband, I forgot to tell you that this Friday I had a *"shvitz"* and you probably don't want to know but I can't know your opinion. I do what I have to do and I'm writing to you because I know you want to know about the *"shvitz."*

[What is interesting about this letter is that in the middle of the paragraph, at the end of the page, Hirsh Zeidberg, who described himself as a "good friend" added a note.]

How much of my grandmother's condition was apparent to my grandfather before he left? Did he dismiss her outbursts as examples of her fiery temperament? Or did his leaving aggravate her already fragile hold on stability?

My cousin Rita who wrote in an email to me that Clara was sent to a sanatorium about twice a year to "calm her nervous condition," confirming that Clara continued to have such episodes throughout her life. According to Rita, Clara remained for a month or two and then was sent home.

If Leib Yosef wrote that Clara was *meshuggah* because he believed that she had mental health problems, then his comments on her behavior seem callous and dismissive. Even if we understand that those with physical and mental difficulties were hidden or shunned at that time, it is difficult to reconcile Leib Yosef's lack of compassion toward his daughter–in-law with the forward-looking way he and Faige Zeisel raised Chana, their physically challenged daughter. Moreover, we would expect that he would be concerned about the well-being of his two grandsons who were left in their mother's care.

If Clara had mental health issues and was under a doctor's treatment, she would have been prevented from immigrating with her sons to the United States. And my grandfather would, of course, have known this. It must have been during this time that Levi and Clara determined that their marriage had to be formally terminated, as she would never be permitted entry to the United States. My grandfather must have obtained a *get*, a decree of divorce according to Jewish law, and sent it to Clara. A cruel blow to her, no doubt, but my grandfather must have concluded that the best hope for his sons' futures lay in their leaving Borchov, not in his returning.

Although Levi was no longer married to Clara, his concern, affection and sense of responsibility for his sons never wavered. He had sent money so that Shlomo and Yisroel could attend *gymnasium*. We have a series of receipts showing that my grandfather regularly sent money back to Borchov. One such receipt shows that he sent $50 to Clara Neuringer on 1 January 1921 via American Express.

Receipt of transfer of money from New York

When Shlomo turned fifteen, putting him close to the age when he could be drafted into the Polish Army, Levi realized he had to move quickly.

Sol Neuringer, my father, at around age 15

This must have been a time of enormous emotional conflict for Shlomo. On the one hand, this was his chance to leave Borchov, a village of ever-diminishing opportunity, for the unlimited horizons of America. But how could he leave his mother and younger brother behind? And what would it be like, living with his father, whom he hadn't seen in ten years?

Along with the few clothes he had, Shlomo packed the last report card he had received from his *gymnasium*, along with his anxieties, doubts and fears. On the station platform, he made firm promises that his brother would follow him as soon as possible and that he would return to visit his mother. Shlomo arrived in New York aboard the SS *Aquitania* on 8 November 1924. In order to gain clearance from Ellis Island, he had to pass a health examination, show that he had $10 in his possession (no doubt supplied by my grandfather) and swear that he was not an anarchist or member of a political party that advocated overthrowing the current United States government. Once admitted, he joined his father who was living in an apartment in the Williamsburg area of Brooklyn.

Five years later, on 24 December 1929, his younger brother, Yisroel, joined him. But the household Yisroel moved into was far different from the one my father had entered. My grandfather had married Ruchel Schneider in February 1928, and they had a son, named Leib Yosef (in Hebrew), born on 20 November 1928. Ruchel was one of his sister Aiga's daughters and, therefore, my grandfather's niece. My brothers, cousins and I have always felt uncomfortable since we discovered this relationship.

In fact, this relationship is perfectly acceptable according to Jewish law. In the book of Leviticus, Chapter 18, verses 12–14, the list of family members who are prohibited from marrying one another is given. Since there is no reference to a man not being able to marry his niece, or a woman her uncle, Jewish law accepts such a relationship. For example, when the editors of *Etz Chaim*, the Torah translation authorized by the Rabbinical Assembly of the United Synagogue of Conservative Judaism and published by the Jewish Publication Society in 2001, wrote the annotation for this verse, they noted that such an arrangement is encouraged, but provided no further explanation for this (Kushner 688).

Once Levi's marriage to Clara was terminated and my father, and a few years later my uncle, joined my grandfather, Aiga might have encouraged a second marriage for her brother, having herself known the challenges of being a single parent. And what better candidate to suggest to her youngest brother than one of her own daughters? We will never know the answer.

How difficult it must have been for my father and uncle to see their older cousin married to their father! Today the adjustment to divorce and remarriage is not an uncommon reality. But in the earlier part of the last century, it was rare, especially within the Jewish community.

Whatever my father and uncle thought of the situation they found in New York, they accorded their father and stepmother the respect their positions required. The fact that the extended Neuringer family accepted this marriage is demonstrated by the standing my grandfather had within the LYN Family Circle (the acronym for the Neuringer family circle). He was the one the others turned to for advice and counsel. Others in the family might have been ostracized or gossiped about for various infractions, but not my grandfather.

My brothers, cousins and I grew up knowing that we had a grandmother living in far-off Europe and a *Tante*

Rosie married to our grandfather. They lived less than ten blocks away with their two children, our young uncle and aunt. As children we never thought to question this unusual family situation.

Levi Neuringer (my grandfather)

And how did my Grandmother Clara react to this turn of events? We have no letters from her or anyone else from either the Neuringer or the Fahrer side of the family that give us any indication of her feelings.

On the one hand she might have been devastated. The *yentas* sitting on the bench were correct: her husband had abandoned her! More humiliating would have been the knowledge that her rival was a younger woman, her former husband's niece, whom Clara had known since birth.

On the other hand, perhaps she had a sense of relief. Having lived for so many years on her own, she might have welcomed the finality of a relationship that had been so stormy and unfulfilling. At that point in her life all she really cared about may have been the love and support – both emotional and financial – that she received from her sons. And this she certainly had.

At this time, back in New York, Levi was beginning to realize his American dream. He had joined in a partnership with two Italian Americans and an Irish American to form the American Casserole and Specialty Company. In an industrial building in the Williamsburg area of Brooklyn, they manufactured patented nickel and brass frames for casseroles, pie plates and candy dishes, as well as serving trays, ashtrays and other giftware.

Once in New York, the other family members found jobs with the assistance of those who had arrived earlier, enrolled in night classes to learn English and in most cases Americanized their names. Levi was signing documents as Louis. Shlomo, whose report card from the *gymnasium* identified him as Salomon, was now known as Sol and his brother, Yisroel, became Irving.

I grew up knowing the brothers Mattityahu and Hirsh as Max and Herman. Haskall became Charlie. His wife, Aiga, was now known as Eva, his daughters Ruchel and Liba became Rosie and Libby and his son, Gershon became George.

As soon as they could afford it, they also shed their Old World clothes for the latest American designs. And so they lived, assimilating where they could, speaking English in the workplace and Yiddish at home, at extended family gatherings and when they met at Borchover Society meetings. Some worked on *Shabbos* when necessary, but kept kosher homes and ate in kosher restaurants when they went out.

In short, while the majority of Borchovers living in New York modified the Jewish way of life to American customs, they kept their Jewish identification rather than melting into the multicultural pot.

Chapter 15:

Borchov Rebuilds

The time for rebuilding Borchov had come once World War I ended. The political map of Europe was redrawn, and the rest of the western part of Galicia was restored to Poland.

Like the rushing waters of the rivers near Borchov that sought quiet ponds and lakes in which to settle, so too swirled crowds of people seeking peace and refuge. Many who had come to Borchov from other communities stayed there because their own shtetls had been destroyed during the war. Those remaining in Borchov resumed their attempts to make a living and to raise and educate their children according to the principles of their religion. For some, such as Goldie's husband, Mendl Gross, business continued; whenever they could, Borchovers bought meat from the butcher.

For the majority of the Jewish community, however, the economic situation deteriorated even further. Now they were facing competition from the Poles and Ukrainians who were beginning to enter trades, such as tailoring and watchmaking, formerly dominated by Jews. No longer would a peasant need to come to Borchov to purchase farm implements from a Jewish merchant; he could obtain what he needed from a Polish or Ukrainian businessman.

At the same time, licensing fees to run a business continued to rise. Pressured on all sides, the small Jewish merchant was often forced to liquidate his business. Not only was he unemployed, but also his son could no longer expect to make his living in the same way that his father had.

We do not know if Clara was able to maintain her business during this period. Cousin Rita reported that once Clara's sons left for America, she regularly received packages from them that allowed her to live "well."

Some tried to adapt to the changing world. Then the area started to be electrified. Some young Jewish men became electricians, climbing the high poles to string wires. Others turned to an old trade that had flourished until World War I: they were smugglers. Because of Borchov's position near the borders of Russia, Ukraine and Romania, there were always those who made their living by bringing in goods illegally.

Manufactured goods, as well as cows and horses, had been brought across the borders clandestinely before the war in order to avoid paying the high taxes imposed both by the Austro-Hungarian Empire and by Russia. This illicit trade resumed after World War I and even created jobs for men who worked as guides and porters.

During the period of Czarist rule in Russia, young Jewish men had been smuggled into Galicia along winding, obscure paths in order to escape being drafted into the Czar's army. Knowledge of the forests and mountains would prove to be lifesaving two decades later when partisans and resistance fighters followed them during World War II to elude Nazi soldiers.

In general, those who remained in Borchov came to realize that there were many reasons they could not go back to living according to the old ways. The practice of having only a religious education changed when Galicia was returned to Polish rule after World War I. An extensive system of "public schools" was developed and became available in Borchov as well as the other small shtetls. Parents could send their children to these schools where Polish was the language of instruction and the curriculum was secular. Many Jewish parents welcomed this because they recognized that the way to higher education and possible entrance into a profession lay in the knowledge of math, sciences and the like. But they still wanted their children to be learned in Torah and the tenets of their Jewish religion.

To counter the solely secular education available in the public schools, in 1924, the Jewish community organized a Talmud Torah for religious instruction to replace the traditional *cheder*. Leib Yosef and Faige Zeisel's grandchildren could go to a public school during the early part of the day and have religious instruction in Hebrew in the afternoon. Since the Talmud Torah opened the same year my father left Borchov, it is not likely he attended it. However, since my uncle did not leave until 1929, it is possible that he was one of the Talmud Torah students. The methods used to teach the children in the new Talmud Torah were modern, and both boys and girls could attend some classes together. Unlike the traditional *cheder*, where the boys sat on long benches, in the Talmud Torah the students sat at school desks.

Although the traditional full-day *cheder* still existed for those who preferred an Orthodox education for their sons, the Borchovers themselves were surprised at how many parents wanted to enroll their children in the new Talmud Torah. Only a few families, however, were able to afford the tuition fees. Consequently, they turned to the Borchover Society in New York for help.

My grandfather was president of the Society at this time. He had transformed from the four-year-old who developed "headaches" to avoid *cheder*, to a teenager who stayed up all night, straining his eyes in the dim light to read and study texts, to a person in a position of authority who could arrange for financial help for the Talmud Torah.

The Society arranged to send one hundred American dollars a year to Borchov to pay the salaries of the two or three teachers who taught there. In addition, the Borchover Jews in America would occasionally send additional money that was used to purchase shoes or clothing for the students.

Naturally, the President of the Talmud Torah wrote effusive letters of thanks to the Borchovers in New York. In 1927 the Society received the following letter, which was quoted in the Yizkor Book:

> If you were here and you would see what we do with the money that you send, how approximately one hundred children learn Torah seriously with good teachers and a good study program in a good location in a Talmud Torah that we built ourselves in 1924, and how the kids can recite [passages from the Talmud and commentaries] orally from memory, you would dance for joy. I'm not writing with exaggeration – God forbid. On the contrary, I am writing even less than it really is.

The Talmud Torah existed until the outbreak of World War II in September 1939. During the years of Soviet rule, from 1939 to 1941, the Soviets turned the building into a workshop for craftsmen. From the German occupation until the liquidation of the Borchov ghetto in June 1943, the Talmud Torah and the *rov's* residence were left vacant.

The writers of the Yizkor Book did not comment on how many young Borchov people were able to pursue higher education in the period between the wars. My father was among the Borchovers who attended the *gymansium* after

World War I. Since the students had to pay tuition for higher education, I can only assume that my grandfather sent money for my father and then my uncle to attend.

The *gymnasium* report card that Shlomo, my father, brought with him to New York in 1924 shows that he had completed the third year of the privately funded co-ed *gymnasium* that was part of the Polish school system of the Tarnopol region. Shlomo had taken ten subjects that school year. Although religion is one of the listed subjects, the report does not specify if he studied his own religion, although he is identified as being Jewish. In any event, his mark is "Good." He also studied German and Polish, with his German mark being the higher of the two. This is not surprising, considering that prior to the end of World War I, any public schooling he had would have been conducted in German. The school also offered courses in Russian and Latin.

In addition to history, geography, mathematics, chemistry and botany, my father also had a class in drawing and manual skills, which I assume is equivalent to our industrial arts or shop class. He received his best mark, "Very Good," in this class. All his other marks were in the "Satisfactory to Good" range.

The hunger for knowledge extended to the adult population of Borchov. In the same year that the Talmud Torah was established, Jewish Borchovers also opened the Czytelnia. This was a combination library/cultural center that was established by a group of Borchovers and did not have financial support from any other organizations.

Unlike a public library, where membership is free, this library required people to pay monthly dues. With the money collected, the organizers were able to purchase thousands of books in Yiddish, Polish, German and Hebrew. As a result many non-Jewish residents – Poles and Ukrainians – also became members of the Czytelnia.

Sol Neuringer and an unidentified man in the library

In the reading room, Shlomo Reibel, who described it for the Yizkor Book, and the other members could choose from approximately fifty newspapers written in Yiddish, Polish, Hebrew, Ukrainian and German. Borchovers could read news and commentaries from Warsaw, Berlin, Tel Aviv, Kiev and possibly even New York City, where the *Jewish Daily Forward* was published in Yiddish.

The Czytelnia was made up of two rented rooms and had a staff of two. It was open every evening and twice a week during the day. As well as being able to borrow books and read newspapers, members could also attend lectures that were given by people who either lived in Borchov or were invited from other places. One of the first lecturers was Nachman Blumenthal, the editor of the Yizkor Book, who gave a series of "Scientific Talks" on Saturday mornings. So many people began coming to these talks, and so great was the interest in all kinds of subjects, that an additional group of lectures was organized for Saturday evenings. In addition, theatrical performances, with both local and visiting actors, were held there.

The Czytelnia existed for fifteen years until the outbreak of World War II. At first, when the Soviet Union invaded Borchov and its surrounding area, the board of the Czytelnia, which included Shlomo Reibel, voted to join other cultural organizations of the Ukrainian community. In this way, they hoped, the library would be able to stay open. However, Reibel later wrote:

> But no one could have imagined that in another two years the Nazis would put an end to all the cultural achievements of the Jewish people in such a horrendous fashion.

Sol's membership "card" for the Czytelnia

In spite of all their efforts to revitalize the town, life continued to be difficult for most of the Jews of Borchov. Leaving, however, was equally difficult as new immigration laws in the United States, Canada and Palestine prevented most applicants from getting visas. Only people who had immediate family already living in those countries could get permission to join them.

There were opportunities for some. Alter Kowalek, the only son of my grandfather's sister Sarah and her husband, Archie, wanted to be a dentist. Jews were beginning to be accepted into medical and other professional schools. However, there was a quota for the number of Jews admitted so that only a small number who applied would gain entry. Those students had to have superior marks. They also needed to be able to afford the tuition fees and the expense of living in one of the larger cities.

Alter was successful in his application to a school of dentistry in Danzig. He left Borchov and traveled north to the Polish city on the Baltic Sea coast. He completed his studies, married and remained there. His four sisters also married but stayed in Borchov.

In the latter part of the 1930s, Sarah, his mother, developed breast cancer. In spite of two operations, she died in 1938. Cousin Rita recalled her mother telling her that Sarah was a very clean, fastidious person, who couldn't bear the thought of being buried directly into the ground according to Orthodox Jewish tradition. Before her death, she requested that she be buried in a casket. Her adoring husband, Archie, honored her wishes.

There was now only one of Faige Zeisel and Leib Yosef's children left living in Borchov; their youngest daughter, Goldie remained.

In 1933, the National Socialist German Workers' Party (the Nazis), headed by Adolph Hitler, was elected to be the governing party in Germany. Immediately this new government began passing stringent laws that restricted the lives of Jews. Jewish lawyers were disbarred and not permitted to practice law, Jewish doctors were no longer granted privileges to work in German hospitals and Jewish professors could no longer teach in universities.

With each day bringing news of further restrictions and new laws passed, the Jewish communities in neighboring countries became more nervous and anxious. The news was becoming more and more ominous. Once again, as it had been in the years before World War I, there was talk of war. The "Great War" was supposed to have been "the war to end all wars." But lasting peace was proving to be an illusion.

I believe that it was at this time that Nachman Blumenthal, his brother Moshe and their families were able to move to Palestine. For wealthier Jews living in the larger cities, it was possible to bribe officials in order to obtain the necessary documents to leave. For the poorer Jews who lived in the isolated shtetls such as Borchov, the possibility of leaving in time was becoming more and more remote.

Chapter 16:

A Return Visit

On 22 March 1933, my father left New York for a six-month visit to Borchov. He was now a handsome young man of twenty-four who had Americanized his name from Shlomo to Sol. After working and saving his money for this journey, he was anxiously looking forward to seeing his mother again. Nine years had passed since he had left his birthplace, and much had happened to both of them.

The family myth is that he was determined to arrange for Clara to return to New York with him. But we do not know if this was true or even possible.

There was an urgency to Sol's voyage. He had been reading reports of Hitler's rise in Germany and of the restrictive laws against Jews that were being enacted there. His memories of growing up in Borchov during World War I with hunger, chaos and disease were still vivid. He did not want his mother to be trapped in Borchov again.

Under the provisions of the Immigration Act of 1924 and its later revisions, my father and uncle might have been able to sponsor their mother as a non-quota immigrant. However, from 1882 on, the Act to Regulate Immigration prohibited entry to "any person unable to take care of him or herself without becoming a public charge." Included on the list of those to be excluded were the mentally ill. This was reaffirmed in 1917. Therefore it is probable that a visa for Clara to immigrate could not have been obtained if her mental condition was still unstable.

Sol also wanted to see his aunts, uncles, cousins and childhood friends who still lived there, and to photograph the shtetl he had left behind. He recorded everything he saw and everyone he met, precisely noting the dates, times and places the pictures were taken. Frustratingly, however, he seldom identified the people in the pictures!

The first set of pictures was taken aboard the ship, mostly on the deck. My father loved being on the water. While others complained of seasickness, cramped conditions, foul weather or poor food, he was invigorated by the tangy salt air, the screeching of sea birds near land and the stimulation of meeting new people. He even relished taking the ferry from Brooklyn across New York's harbor to Staten Island.

The crossing aboard the SS *Manhattan* from New York to the first European port took eight days. The ship first docked in the port of Le Havre, France. From Le Havre, the SS *Manhattan* sailed north, turning into the mouth of the Elbe River and then to the port of Hamburg in northern Germany a day later. When the ship sailed into Hamburg's harbor, Sol observed the German naval vessels docked nearby. He knew that these had been built in violation of the terms of disarmament that had been set down by the League of Nations following World War I. His apprehension was heightened.

One of the last pictures taken aboard the ship, dated 31 March 1933, shows Sol standing on the deck, facing the camera. He is wearing a tweed overcoat, a fashionable fedora, long, dark pants and what look like suede gloves. The former shtetl dweller had been transformed into a modern, urban young man. In the vernacular of the day, he could be described as "dapper" or "dashing." After reading the letters that described the criticism Clara had faced for dressing so *farpitzed* after my grandfather left, I wonder what the Borchov gossips said about my father's wardrobe!

Sol Neuringer on board ship

A clue to a possible reaction was given by Shlomo Reibel in the Yizkor Book. In his chapter on leisure time activities of pre–World War I Borchov, Reibel described the impact of visitors from outside the area. The visitors would be invited into people's homes to tell stories of the places they had seen. Included in this group were traveling merchants, visitors from Eretz Yisroel who came to empty the *pushkas* and "an American Jew who came back from America with a fedora on his head and coins in his pocket."

From Hamburg, Sol took a train, probably to Warsaw and then on to Lvov, which at that time was known as Lemberg and was in Poland. There he spent a few days with a friend whom he identifies only as "N." I believe that this may have been Nachman Blumenthal. Letters exchanged with Nachman's brother, Moshe, in 1960, indicate that the men were friends.

They visited the public park in Lemburg and had a meal in a restaurant, where Sol is shown reading a newspaper that was spread out over a wooden rack, as papers still are in the cafes of Europe. In the photograph, Sol is wearing a three-piece suit. Another picture was taken in front of the University of Lemburg. Was Nachman a student there?

The two friends went to the theatre on 17 April. Sol noted that it was the biggest theatre in Poland. They saw a performance of *Fraulein Doctor*.

For me, the most intriguing pictures from Sol's visit to Lemburg are the two taken of a pair of men in military uniform. One picture is of Sol, Nachman and the two uniformed men; the second is of the men alone with Sol. According to the captions my father wrote on the back of the two photographs, I learned that these men, one a captain, the other a corporal, were "Jewish Fascists called 'Trumpeldor'" who were on their way to Palestine. There is no explanation of how Sol knew them; if they were not Borchovers, perhaps Nachman knew them from living in Lemburg.

Finally, almost a month after he left New York, Sol boarded a train for Borchov. Sol must have noticed that not much of the rhythm of daily life as he had experienced it had changed. Yosef Hirsh was still leading his horse through the streets and back lanes of the shtetl, bringing water to the residents. As before, there were people living on the outskirts of Borchov who penned goats in their yards in order to get milk. The streets were still either unpaved or paved roughly with cobblestones.

Sol and a friend at the river

When he wanted to visit a nearby village, Sol could, as before, hire a horse-drawn wagon to take him there. And on a hot summer's day, he and his friends would gather on the banks of the Nichtawa River. As he walked down the slope toward the river, he might have recalled that going to the river as a child often meant running past a gauntlet of non-Jewish boys who would jeer, curse and even throw stones at him. Now those young boys were also young men who were too busy making their own livings to bother harassing the groups of Jews. Besides, they knew that the next day, Sunday, their day of rest, they could go to the same spot to swim. But he had no doubt that they maintained their anti-Semitic feelings.

Although there are numerous pictures recording Sol's visit with his friends and relatives, there is not one picture of him and Clara together. I find this puzzling, unless she was in a sanatorium during the time of his visit.

While in Borchov, Sol took out a temporary membership in the Czytelnia so that he could read the newspapers and meet his friends. The debate about whether to stay or leave Borchov still raged. With the United States and Canada tightening immigration rules and numbers, the choices were becoming limited. Sol may have known of one distant Neuringer cousin who went to Buenos Aires with his family; he had been denied entry to the United States even though his brothers were already living in New Jersey.

While Sol was in Borchov, he surely showed his mother pictures of a lively young woman he'd met, Dorothy Horowitz, whom he planned to marry. Her parents came from Chortkiev and Husiatyn, shtetls near Borchov, although Dotty (as she was known), her brother and three sisters were born in New York.

Sol also told his mother that when he returned, he and his brother Irving planned to open a store in Brooklyn, selling floor coverings.

If it was Sol's intention to arrange for his mother to return to New York with him, he did not meet with success. Despite assurances that she would be welcomed, loved and cared for in New York, either she would not or could not leave Borchov.

On a morning early in August, Sol once again boarded a train to leave Borchov. After retracing his steps through Lemberg to Hamburg, he boarded the SS *Roosevelt,* arriving in

New York's harbor on 18 August 1933.

In his suitcase were rolls of film – the pictures he'd snapped to record his visit and show to his family and the other Borchovers in New York. He was also carrying some gifts his mother had given him for his bride: a metal mortar and pestle set for grinding spices and a small tray holding a decanter and six stemmed goblets for schnapps. These were placed in our living room, always displayed in a place of honor, along with Clara's picture. Grandma Clara, a handsome woman, whose features were clearly like my father's; Grandma Clara, the grandmother I never met and about whom I know so little.

How wrenching Sol's leaving must have been this time! When he left Borchov the first time, the source of his apprehension was that he was going toward the unknown. He was going to live with a father that he had not seen for ten years. Now, he knew where he was going; his fear was for those he was leaving behind.

Chapter 17:

World War II Begins

World War II officially began on a Friday, 1 September 1939, when the Nazi German Army invaded Poland. Shlomo Reibel, writing about the war for the Yizkor Book, recalled that at first the mood in Borchov was calm. People reasoned that the rest of the world would unite and destroy Hitler's armies, and that would be the end of him.

The optimistic mood changed quickly with the news that the Polish army was retreating. This was followed by warnings that the Soviet army was approaching Borchov. As at the beginning of World War I, Borchov was occupied by an army from the east. Incredibly, the Soviets had signed a peace pact with Hitler's government!

For a year and a half, life in Borchov remained relatively calm. There were hardships, of course, as food became scarce and people had to line up for bread and other meager rations. In addition, there was a news blackout, so no one knew what was happening to Jews living in other countries.

Despite all this, as unbelievable as it seems, we have two letters that Clara wrote to her son, my Uncle Irv, in late winter and early spring of 1941.

The first, dated 22/II 1941, acknowledges a letter and Hannukah present she received from Clara's "faithful son Yisrultzi['s]...dear son..." She is referring to my cousin who was born on 6 October 1940. She continued, "...you ask me how I am, how I'm managing with what you send me. I write you that everything is okay. I can't write everything."

I wonder if this comment is an indication that she suspected that the mail was being censored. She went on:

> I'm very anxious to know how things are with you. Now the Pesach season is starting so I wish you, my dear children, a happy season and I also wish you a happy Pesach. Nothing else is important, my dear faithful children: be well and happy. I send warm regards, kisses to each of you. I send warm regards and kiss my two dear students, may they be well and content.

Were her "two dear students" her sons who left Borchov in their teens when they were *gymnasium* students? Her next sentence mentioned her grandchildren, including me, for I was born two years before my cousin:

> Now I kiss thousands of times my dear grandchildren. May they be well and grow with much *mazel*. Amen. May God grant that they should not know any misfortune and may you be protected from all bad news.
>
> Your faithful and good wishing mother who hopes to yet see you in good health and happiness. I kiss you many times, Chaiki.
>
> Don't forget, my dear children...

Here her letter ended abruptly, and it is possible that a third page was lost in the intervening years. What is most poignant about this letter is her hope to "yet see you." Rather than understanding this as an indication of her denial of her situation, I read this as an expression of a mother's love, extending to her children a thread of hope and optimism.

I was immeasurably touched upon learning that she knew about me. No doubt my father and uncle had sent her pictures;

in her next letter, she wrote of the "…lovely and beautiful children…."

So much of Clara's life consisted of unhappiness and separations; at least she had the vicarious pleasure of knowing about her young grandchildren.

That next letter, dated 16 April 1941, was written after Pesach:

My dearly beloved and faithful children,
I am well and hope to hear good news from you. Amen.

Now, my dear children, I received a letter from you that made me very happy. It contained a picture of your dear son, may he be well and have much *mazel*. Amen. He is just as beautiful as you when you were a child. May God grant that you and your dear brother "Lumzi" should have much *naches* from your lovely and beautiful children. And may God grant that I should be well together with you.

Now, dear son "Yisrultznya" you write that [there is a] draft. This causes me great worry and I pray to God to protect you from being drafted and may no misfortune fall upon you. And may God grant that it should be peaceful.

What anxiety news of the draft must have given Clara. All her life, she perceived being drafted as the worst possible thing that could happen to a young man. She must have recalled the numbers of men who made their way over the mountains to avoid being drafted into the Czar's army or the methods used by Borchovers to keep their sons from going into the Emperor's army during World War I.

The irony must have escaped her, for had her son been drafted, he would have fought on the side that was trying to defeat the Soviet Union and Nazi Germany. As it turned out, neither my uncle nor my father were called up because they both had children.

Her letter continued:

> Summer is approaching. Now dear beloved son, Yisrultznya, as I write this letter the postman brought me a letter from you and a five-dollar bill was enclosed. May you be well and may God help you to be successful with all good things and protect your every step from anything bad. Amen.
>
> Also, dear son, Yisrultznya, you write in your letter that you had my photo enlarged. You did the right thing. May God help you by rewarding you and may we be worthy of being together in good health and with great pleasure.
>
> All winter long I have been cooking myself and I made Pesach myself. And may God help me further. Nothing more of importance. May you, my dear and faithful children be well and strong and may God protect you from all evil. And may you be blessed on every step because faithful children as you are, are not to be found in the whole world. I send you regards and kiss you heartily. Special regards and kisses to my dear, lovely daughters-in-law and the two sweet grandchildren. May they grow with great *mazel*. Amen. Your faithful mother, who wishes you well. I hope to see you in good health and happiness. I kiss you numberless times.
>
> Chaiki

She signed her letter neither with any form of "Mother," as might be expected when writing to her son, nor with "Clara" as she closed her letters to my grandfather. "Chaiki" is a diminutive of her Yiddish name, Chaika. Why did she sign off this way? Is she using a name that may recall her childhood, a name that reverts to a happier, carefree time of her life? Or was this name my uncle used to call her? In either case, it elicits a sense of warmth and closeness between mother and son.

How different this is from the postscript Faige Zeisel wrote to Levi in the letter Leib Yosef wrote on 26 April 1914. The earlier letter is a plea for a son to send money to his mother who is in dire straits. Clara's position was no less dire, yet she reassured her son that she had been cooking and made Pesach, and that she had "the best children in the world."

At the bottom of the page, in a different handwriting, someone else wrote, "Regards to the whole family. For the time being, everything is all right by us."

The tone of this last letter is elegiac, resigned. Clara was sixty years old by that time. Gone was the feisty tone of the earlier letters. Although she continued to sound hopeful and reassuring to her sons, I suspect that she understood that she would not be able to write to them much longer, and that she was summing up her love and feeling for them. She did not burden them with her concerns about her situation or the future. Beneath her seeming calm, I suspect that she sensed that life in Borchov is becoming darker, in spite of the arrival of spring.

Chapter 18:
The Nazis Arrive

Hitler's armies invaded the Soviet Union in June 1941. The Soviet Army retreated from Borchov and many families decided to pack up and leave with them. At this time there were approximately 3,000 Jews remaining in Borchov. Ukrainian officials took over governing the shtetl, and a squad of Ukrainian Auxiliary Police remained in Borchov even after the Nazis arrived.

Shlomo Reibel's entry in the Yizkor Book described what occurred next. Within a few months the Nazi army arrived, bringing with them the oppressive laws against the Jews that they had proclaimed in other occupied European countries. The first order was that Jews had to identify themselves by wearing on their right arms a white armband with a blue *Magen David* on it.

Then, Jews between the ages of fourteen and sixty were required to work for the Germans. Another law defined the hours Jews could be out on the streets. They could shop in the market only from noon to one o'clock. They could not travel away from their home villages without a special permit. Jewish schools and businesses were closed. Jewish students were prohibited from attending the public schools.

Newspapers and magazines no longer came in from outside the shtetl. The few Jews who might have had radios had to turn them in to the Nazi authorities. With no news coming in from the outside world, Borchovers had no way of knowing what was happening to family and friends in other communities or, indeed, what other countries were engaged in the war.

Just as Borchovers had no way of getting news from outside the area, neither had those living in unoccupied countries any news of events in Borchov. In New York, Aiga was frantic with worry about the fate of Rifke, her daughter, her son-in-law and grandchildren.

Alter Kowalek, Sarah's son, who was then living in another part of Poland, was unable to contact his father, Archie, or his sisters who were still in Borchov. Alter and his wife went into hiding in Poland.

To Shlomo Reibel, living in Borchov was like living in a cage, a cage that was getting smaller and smaller as the Nazi soldiers began to create a ghetto in April 1942. The designated area where Jews were to live was confined to some of the poorer streets.

It was an "open ghetto." No barbed wire or fences surrounded these streets. Jews were informed that if they strayed outside the permitted area, they could be arrested or shot. It is probable that Goldie, Faige Zeisel and Leib Yosef's last surviving daughter, and her husband Mendl Gross had to move from the home that was such a source of Mendl's pride, leaving behind the furniture Goldie had dusted and polished all those years.

Since we do not know exactly where in Borchov my grandmother was living, we do not know if my Grandmother Clara was among those who were forced to move. Although contact between Jews and non-Jews was prohibited, Goldie and Mendl and others like them who had goods to barter were able to survive by selling their possessions to non-Jews who smuggled food into the ghetto at great peril to themselves. If they were discovered, they too could be arrested and sent to the labor camps that were set up in the forest outside of Borchov.

Since my grandmother was living on funds sent by my father and uncle and that source was no longer available, we do not know how she managed to live. Unlike other parts of Poland and Europe, the Nazis did not round up large numbers of Jews in Borchov for transport to concentration camps. However, younger men and some women were sent to forced labor camps. Rather, in this area of Galicia and Ukraine, Nazi policy was to round up Jews, march them to the forest beyond the shtetl or to the cemetery, and shoot the people there. These were known as *Aktions*.

After the first *Aktion* of 26–27 September 1942, surviving Jews from neighboring villages were forced to move to Borchov. This increased the population to 4,000. On 1 December 1942, the ghetto was "closed;" barbed wire was strung up, separating it from the rest of the shtetl. Hunger and disease spread throughout the crowded area.

It is probable that members of Leib Yosef and Faige Zeisel's family perished in these *Aktions*. My grandfather wrote that Minnie, one of his sister Chana's daughters, died along with her husband and children.

Calling the Nazis "wild beasts in the form of humans," Levi also recorded that Rifke, Aiga's eldest daughter, was also killed along with her husband and most of her children. One of Rifke's daughters, Faige Zeisel, did survive.

Except for her son, Alter, hiding in Poland, the same fate befell Sarah's husband, children and grandchildren. None of Goldie and Mendl's children survived.

We do have a chilling description of the third such *Aktion*, written by Yakov Schwartz and published in the Yizkor Book. As I read his heart-stopping account, I wondered where my grandmother was on that fateful day.

Schwartz wrote that the *Aktion* took place on a Monday in April 1943, the eve of Pesach. He remembered how frightened and anxious people were, certain that another *Aktion* would probably take place soon, but of course they had no information about the exact date.

Yakov was sitting outside of his brother-in-law's house with his six-year-old son Shmulik. He never allowed Shmulik out of his sight since his wife, two daughters and a younger son had been deported the previous *Succos* along with many other members of his family. Yakov was observing the activity taking place in the market just beyond the ghetto street. The non-Jews were buying food for their Easter celebrations. Yakov and his sister-in-law recognized a man they knew who had brought a basket of eggs to sell in the market. They smuggled him into the ghetto area and bought the eggs. In spite of their desperate situation, they were able to joke that they needed the eggs to celebrate Pesach. They were recalling how, in normal times, Yakov's sister-in-law would have been very busy that day cooking and preparing for the *seder* that night.

All of a sudden, as the clock in the church tower struck noon, Yakov's sister-in-law began shouting, "Run away! People are running for some reason!"

They heard shots. In his account, Yakov wrote that he found it impossible to describe the scene. Hundreds of people were running in panic through the narrow streets of the ghetto, trying to find places to hide.

Yakov grabbed Shmulik and began running toward the *shul*. He knew that beyond the *shul*, which was at the edge of the ghetto, was an open field with tall grasses and bushes. Yakov had hidden there before. This day, however, the street was blocked by two Gestapo holding their guns, so Yakov turned and ran in another direction, dragging Shmulik with him. Frantically looking to find a place to hide, Yakov pulled Shmulik into a house he knew was empty. Miraculously, there was a ladder in the middle of the room that led to the attic above. He shoved Shmulik up the rungs, climbed up behind him and, without thinking, dragged the ladder up and closed the trap door of the attic.

Yakov and Shmulik crawled into a corner of the attic, covering their bodies with a dusty blanket and their feet with a sack of old clothes they found lying on the floor.

Father and son remained hidden in the attic, hearing the cries as relatives, neighbors and friends were dragged out of their hiding places. They lay that way for the rest of the day and through the night, without food or water. The church clock kept telling them the hour and half hour. Finally, at ten o'clock the next morning, hearing no sounds from the street below, Yakov knew that he had to leave the attic to find water for Shmulik, who was dangerously dehydrated, his lips cracked and parched. Slowly, carefully, he eased the attic door open, taking no risks that it would creak or squeak.

Just as he was about to put the ladder down he heard a conversation in Polish coming from the room below. He recognized the voice of a Nazi policeman, Lange, talking to the young Polish girl who worked as a maid for him.

The two were discussing the possibility of finding supplies in the house because a number of Jewish families had been living there. As quietly as he could, Yakov crawled back under the blanket and motioned to Shmulik not to speak or move.

Yakov listened to the footsteps of the maid and the policeman as they searched the house. When they could not find anything of value in the downstairs rooms, the maid noticed the opening in the ceiling leading to the attic and told Lange that is where they would find goods.

Yakov heard Lange, the policeman, push a table under the entrance to the attic. Next he heard a bang as Lange placed a chair on the table and his grunts as he began climbing up. Yakov put his hand over Shmulik's mouth. They held their breaths, as Lange grabbed the sack of old clothes, spilling them out on the floor. Finding a piece of leather, Lange let out a happy cry and climbed down from the attic. Then he and the maid left the house.

Yakov and Shmulik began breathing again; they stayed still a while longer. Shmulik let out a weak moan. Yakov could tell that Shmulik was about to faint from thirst, so he carried his son down from the attic in the same way that Lange had come up: onto the chair and then the table.

Once outside, Yakov went to the nearest water pump and gave the first cup that he pumped out of the well to Shmulik. After they both drank deeply, they heard the clock in the church tower strike noon. The streets around them were silent and empty; twenty-four hours after it began, the Pesach *Aktion* had ended. Years later they would learn that over 3,500 Jews had been killed in Borchov and surrounding villages in that *Aktion*.

Yakov and Shmulik rested for a while, warmed by the early spring sunshine. They listened to some birds singing in the tree that shaded the pump, chirping cheerfully. Then Yakov rose. Taking Shmulik's hand, he began to walk through the narrow, winding streets of the ghetto area, looking for others who had survived. Among those who survived that terrible night was my Grandmother Clara.

It is coincidence, of course, but Pesach, the festival when Jews recall and celebrate their freedom from the tyranny of Pharaoh's Egypt, continually appears as a marker in my grandparents' lives.

The first occurrence was in 1914, when my great grandparents, Leib Yosef and Faige Zeisel, tried to persuade my grandfather not to leave Borchov before Pesach. Clara later wrote to Levi, describing how my father recited the Four Questions.

The next marker was the last letter of my grandmother's, written after Pesach in 1941. She wrote that she had celebrated the holiday alone and was looking forward to spring.

Finally, the *Aktion* chillingly portrayed in the Yizkor Book took place on Pesach eve. We must remember to note this when we sit at our family *seder* each year.

Chapter 19:
Resistance

Not all Borchovers were resigned to surviving as best they could within the confines of the ghetto. According to the account in the Yizkor Book, there was a group of young Borchovers who vowed to do whatever they could to resist the Nazi occupation. By October 1941, they had organized themselves into four groups of five men and five women each. They concluded that it would be better to work separately so that if any group was captured the others could carry on. They called themselves the *Borchover Bande*, meaning the Borchover Gang.

Among them was Lioveh, a Jewish soldier who had fought in the army of the Soviet Union. Although the Nazis had captured him, he managed to escape from the prisoner-of-war camp where he'd been held and make his way to Borchov. He decided to stay there when he met up with the *Borchover Bande*.

Their first task was to find a supply of arms and ammunition. They were able to buy some from sympathetic non-Jews. Other Jews in the shtetl had contacts with the local police, some of whom offered support. Finally, a lieutenant from the Soviet army named Kolya, who was stationed in Borchov when the Soviets had occupied the shtetl at the outbreak of the war, was able to smuggle some arms to the Jewish resisters.

These groups did whatever they could to damage the Nazi war efforts. They blew up railway bridges and derailed trains carrying soldiers and supplies or taking Jews to labor or concentration camps. Once they even managed to blow up the railway yard in a nearby town. Another of these groups shot Lange, the Nazi policeman, a short time after the Pesach Massacre. B.W. Ben-Barak was in one of these resistance groups and later wrote about his experiences for the Yizkor Book. He described how a group of twenty-eight men and women stole out of Borchov on the night of 7 June 1943. After many *Aktions*, there were few Jews left in the ghetto and it had become too dangerous for them to remain in there.

The group made its way into the forest where the members joined others who were already living there in mud huts. Some peasants who lived in the area gave them food; at times their ration was three potatoes per day. It is unclear in the Yizkor Book whether the ration was three per person or three to be shared by the group.

Ben-Barak wrote of one escapade they carried out. In the middle of a late summer's night, they attacked the Nazi soldiers who were guarding the barracks in a neighboring shtetl. Ben-Barak and the other members of his resistance group pounced upon the Nazi guards, bound and gagged them and took their uniforms and arms before stealing away back into the forest.

They waited until the night of 17 November to use the uniforms and guns. The group had heard that approximately 500 Nazi soldiers had been sent to Borchov for a short leave from the front lines.

Assuming that each soldier would not be able to recognize all the others, some of Ben-Barak's group put on the stolen Nazi uniforms. Two others pretended that they were prisoners. The group marched boldly into Borchov and up to the jail. They knew that late at night there would be only one guard on duty.

After pounding on the entrance door, they demanded to be let in with their "prisoners." When the guard opened the door, they overpowered him, gagged him, grabbed his keys and opened up all the cells, freeing approximately forty prisoners. The prisoners, both Jewish and non-Jewish, were able to escape.

Naturally, the Nazi command would not permit this raid to go unpunished. From the information gained from some Jewish prisoners who were recaptured and a few non-Jewish peasants who lived near the forest, the Nazis were able to find out where the resistance group's camp was. The camp was encircled by Nazi troops on 6 December 1943. One of the resistance fighters killed in that raid was Itzia Neuringer. I do not know how he is related to me, but I assume that anyone with the surname Neuringer coming from Borchov somehow is.

The leader of the resistance group divided the survivors into those who had some arms and those who did not. Ben-Barak, along with those who had no arms, was told to run deep into the forest to try and save himself.

Along with four women, Ben-Barak made his way to a small bunker they had dug into the ground at an earlier time, and there they remained through the winter. They were helped by a Polish peasant, Pietr Glud, who brought them food when he could. As the fighting between the Nazi and Soviet armies came closer to their bunker in the forest, Pietr Glud led them to his farm one dark night. There he hid them in his potato cellar.

In March 1944, the Soviet army defeated the Nazi army in that area. Ben-Barak and the four women were free to leave, and they made their way through the forest, back to Borchov. They were the only ones of their resistance group to survive. When the war ended, Ben-Barak went to Israel where he lived for the rest of his life.

Chapter 20:

The Shattered Stones

There was jubilation throughout Europe and the rest of the world when Hitler's armies surrendered to the Allies on 6 May 1945. People danced and cheered in the streets of Paris, London, New York, Jerusalem and Tel Aviv.

In Jewish communities around the world, this joy was tempered by the shocking revelation of the magnitude of their loss. Six million had died in the death camps of Auchwitz and Treblinka, in the ghettos of Warsaw, Vilna and Borchov, and in the fields and forests of the countryside. One and a half million of the dead were children.

The immediate task of the Borchover Societies in New York and Palestine was to find out who had survived and where those people were and to assist them in any way they could. Among my earliest memories is going to a Sunday afternoon meeting of the "organization" to which my father and all the other Neuringer relatives belonged. There I would meet my grandfather and uncles as well as assorted cousins. The formal name of the organization was the *Ershte Borszczower K.U.V.* (or the First Borchover Sick Benefit Society.)

The monthly meetings were held in a building on West 44th Street in Manhattan that had been built expressly to rent rooms for such purposes. The rectangular rooms were designed to replicate a miniature parliament with rows of seats along the longer sides and larger leather armchairs on the shorter sides where the executive members sat and conducted the meetings.

Sometime during World War II my father became the chair

of the Sunshine Fund, which was initially established after World War I for a similar purpose.

The efforts of the committee began while the war still raged in Europe. My father wrote hundreds of letters to organizations such as the Red Cross and the Hebrew Immigrant Aid Society (HIAS) asking for information about relatives and friends. Slowly, responses trickled back to New York. Most of the news was devastating.

One of the earliest letters my father received informed him of his own mother's death; I remember my father's anguished face after he read the letter. It was only recently that I learned how she died.

It was my cousin Rita who was able to tell me that my grandmother had been shot, not in an *Aktion*, but while walking on the street one night after curfew. It was during the time of year when she should have been in the sanatorium, but because of the war that was impossible. Rita's mother told her that Clara had walked up to a Nazi, asked for a light for her cigarette and been shot on the spot.

After my father learned about his mother's fate, he said *kaddish* in her memory and, along with his brother, Irv, purchased a stone bench and had it engraved with her name, Clara Neuringer, and the date of her death, 21 October 1943. The bench stands at the entrance to the Neuringer family burial plot in Beth David Cemetery in Elmont, New York.

Aiga, who had died in 1942, never learned that her daughter, Rifke, was killed with her husband and children. The family, along with a few hundred other people, had been running through the woods to escape an *Aktion*. Rifke was captured by the Nazis, who beat her to death; other members of the family were shot. Only one daughter, Faige Zeisel, named for her great grandmother, survived. Faige Zeisel, her husband Meyer Kowalek and daughter, Rita, were one of the families sponsored by the Sunshine Fund so that they could travel to New York in 1949.

Only one of Chana's daughters, Charni, survived, along with her husband and two married daughters. Charni's sister, Minnie, perished with her family.

Alter Kowalek, Sarah's son, was the only one left from his family. He and Fanya, his wife, survived by acquiring false papers that identified them as Polish. They hid in the small towns of Poland during the war. Eventually, documents were assembled and they, with their son and daughter, were given visas permitting them to travel to New York. My grandfather wrote in his memoir that Shlomo's son Shmuel, who survived the wounds he received during World War I, did not live through World War II. Perhaps Itzia Neuringer, who is listed in the Yizkor Book as having been killed in the forests with other members of his resistance group, in December 1943, was one of his sons. Goldie, her husband, her six children and all of her grandchildren also perished.

Most of those who survived had hidden in the forests or fields. They lived in pits, holes, dugouts or bunkers. A few were saved by sympathetic non-Jews who hid them under the stoves in their houses or in the stalls and haystacks of their barns.

Traumatized by their experiences, their health fragile, their families decimated, their homes destroyed or taken over by non-Jewish neighbors, the remnants of these Eastern European Jewish communities sought shelter in friendly lands. Only a handful wanted to return to Borchov. This time there would be no attempt to rebuild the Jewish community there.

Those who were able to make contact with the US or British forces were taken to displaced persons camps that were established in their zones of Occupied Germany when the war ended. Other camps were established in Austria and Italy. In the camps, the survivors were fed, clothed, given medical attention and offered assistance to assemble the myriad documents needed to resettle in a welcoming country.

Shlomo Reibel was one of those surviving Borchovers who went to a displaced persons camp in the US Zone. From the camp, Reibel wrote to his old friend, Sol Neuringer, in New York. After receiving Shlomo Reibel's first letter in August 1947, my father arranged for three packages of food and clothes to be sent through Cooperative for American Remittances to Europe (CARE), an organization created for such purposes in 1945.

Finally, sometime in 1948, after the State of Israel was declared, Reibel was able to travel there. Yakov Schwartz, his son Shmulik and B.W. Ben-Barak also chose to move to Israel, where they were welcomed by Borchovers already living there, such as Nachman and Moshe Blumenthal.

The New York Borchover Society worked with American immigration agencies to obtain the necessary documents to sponsor Alter Kowalek, his wife and children, and Rifke's daughter, Faige Zeisel, and her husband and children so that they could travel to and settle in the United States. A few other surviving Borchovers were admitted to Canada and went to Montreal, which at that time had the country's largest Jewish community.

Levi Neuringer sat down at his desk in his apartment in Brooklyn, New York, and began writing a history of his family in Yiddish so that his children and grandchildren would know their ancestry. His anguish over the deaths of his sister, brothers-in-law, nieces, nephews and their children at the hands of "the Hitler Beasts," as he called them, aggravated his heart condition, and he died on 25 October 1950 before he had the opportunity to complete his memoir.

After the war ended, non-Jews living in Borchov tore down many of the houses that had belonged to Jews. In one area they planted a small garden with a few trees and some benches. They surrounded the garden with a fence made from monument stones taken from the Jewish cemeteries.

By 1954 there were only three Jews living in Borchov who had lived there in 1939 when the war began. There are no Jews living in Borchov today. The village is now part of the Republic of Ukraine.

Around 1958, some of the Borchovers living in Israel began organizing the writing of the *Book of Borchoff*. Under the editorship of Nachman Blumenthal, these men and women undertook to describe their lives in that small shtetl, to preserve their memories before the passage of time covered them with cobwebs.

The New York Society was expected to assist them by raising funds to underwrite the cost and committing to purchase a set number of books upon publication. Once again, my father was given the responsibility for this. It was no easy task. Many of the New York *landsmen* had no desire to recall their birthplace. In a letter to Nachman Blumenthal's brother Moshe, dated 30 November 1960, Sol described his fundraising efforts:

> Since March 1926, that is to say, nearly 35 years, a very few – and I must point out, not wealthy people – Borchover *landsleit*, undertook to help the needy

back home. For 35 years they worked and sweated and put in a lot of energy and effort – went around to collect for Talmud Torah, for clothes for Pesach for the poor folks – I say <u>went</u> because at that time the Borchover did not yet own an automobile – they trod through snow, frost and in great summer heat calling upon the *landsleit.* (They didn't have telephones either because that was a great luxury.) So they knocked at the doors to awaken the Jewish feeling in their hearts to give – half a dollar – a dollar – two dollars and five dollars was a large contribution. They did that not for publicity but because the Jewish heart cried for the fate of the suffering ones. Many years they were shamed – many people mocked them and some even insulted them.

For 35 years a few New York Borchover *landsleit* sought a way of making the young ones understand [when they would ask] "Why are you working so hard? Why are you putting forth so much effort? Maybe you are gaining something materially from these collections?" But all these expressions did not hold them back from their work.

In your letter you write, "The rich Americans can surely pay $25 for a book."

I can inform you that we have no "rich Americans" – they are only rich in good heartedness. There are indeed Borchover in New York, Canada, Germany and Israel who earn comfortable, good incomes, and a few of them are actually rich. But to get a few dollars from them to support others – God forbid…

Nevertheless after all the trials and tribulations, the Yizkor Book was finally published at the end of 1960.

Chapter 21:

The Scattered Seeds

I once asked my father, "Daddy, when you were a little boy, what did you want to be when you grew up?"

I must have been in high school when I asked my father this question. I don't remember what prompted it, but can picture us sitting in the loft office of his store, perched high over the sales floor, where we could look out over the rolls of broadloom and cases of tiles.

"Be?" my father repeated, "What did I *want* to be? I just wanted to be." If I thought the answer unusual, I didn't pursue the subject further, but as the years have passed, and I raised my own children and watched my grandchildren grow, both generations able to choose how they want to live their lives as adults, my father's response has resonated more and more.

Living under stress, concerned for their immediate survival through a war, my father, uncle and those growing up in Borchov at that time forged their skills of adaptability, determination, persistence and resourcefulness. These were the attributes they carried with them when they finally were able to immigrate to America. Perhaps because there were so few role models for them to want to emulate, they were more open to the variety of jobs and opportunities they found upon arrival to the *goldene medina*.

For them, the future was determined, not by training, higher education or apprenticeship, but by the immediate need to find a job.

The first Neuringers who arrived in New York established businesses that thrived sufficiently after initial struggles, so that their children could seek the higher education they craved but could not afford.

My brothers and I still have a few pieces of giftware from our parents' home that came from the factory that my grandfather and his partners established.

The factory was in an old loft building, and I recall visiting it and riding up the freight elevator: an open wooden platform, raised by an elaborate pulley system. One of the special treats of visiting Grandpa there was stopping on the second floor on the way down. On this floor there was a pickle factory, and I was permitted to put my hand into the brine of a wooden barrel, pull out a crunchy pickle reeking of garlic and chomp away. This, of course, was in the days before rigid health and sanitary rules came into effect. To this day, I am able to only eat kosher dill pickles of a particular taste and flavor, a good thing when watching one's sodium intake is paramount!

For some unexplained reason, many of the younger immigrant Neuringer boys – my father, Uncle Irv, and some of their first cousins who were Yeheskal's sons – went into the floor-covering business. My father and uncle opened a store in the Bensonhurst area of Brooklyn, selling linoleum for the kitchens of the neighborhood and area rugs for the living rooms and bedrooms of the apartments. Post war, as styles changed, they added tiles and wall-to-wall broadloom to their inventory to furnish the single-family houses people were moving into farther out in the suburbs.

Levi's youngest son, Leo, born in the United States, and Yeheskal's youngest son, Joseph, also American born, were able to pursue higher education. Their ambitions soared, and both received their doctorates in physics.

It is the grandchildren who reaped the benefits of the openness of American society toward educational opportunity. It is the generation of grandchildren who studied medicine, history and psychology, becoming professors, elementary school teachers, architects and business people in the new fields of electronics and data processing. From the teenager who had to leave school in order to help his family make a living, to grandchildren strolling the paths of Harvard or Columbia Universities, the dream has been fulfilled.

Today, living in a suburb of New York, there is a young man whose Hebrew name is Leib Yosef, named for his grandfather, who was named for *his* grandfather. There are two Charles Neuringers living in different US cities. They are cousins, both named for their grandfather, Yeheskal.

My son and one of my nephews are named for their grandfather, Sol Neuringer, who was named for his uncle, Shlomo, who died over a century ago in Borchov.

Although the descendants of Leib Yosef and Faige Zeisel live in cities all across the United States and Canada, their names connect them to their family history. From Boston to Florida, to Kansas City, Texas, Oregon and California, Neuringers live, work, raise their children and grandchildren, attend their synagogues and contribute to charitable organizations, both Jewish and secular.

My brothers and I are grandparents now, as are most of our cousins. In recent years there has been a veritable baby boom on the paternal and maternal sides of the family. The babies will be nurtured, grow and attend school, studying subjects unknown and unimagined during my grandfather's and father's day. Being Jewish will not be a barrier that forces them to rule out choices and aspirations. The generations continue and the promise that the New World offered has been fulfilled.

Epilogue

If this story were a traditional fairy tale, it would conclude with the handsome prince and his beautiful princess overcoming their many challenges and obstacles. The final words would be "And they lived happily ever after."

Another variation of a fairy tale would have the evil stepmother getting her deserved punishment, as would all the other villains the hero and heroine had encountered.

Alas, my grandparents' story is not a fairy tale. They were real people, complex individuals trapped by their own personalities and the historical events of the time. The stepmother in this story, Ruchel, was not evil, did not attempt to prevent the two older sons from taking their rightful place in their father's home. In fact, we do not know what precipitated this second marriage.

Neither can we readily identify a villain in this family story. (Yes, the Nazis are universally accepted as hideous villains, but I'm not including them in the accounting of what happened within the family.) Was my grandfather the family villain? We do not have his side of the story; we do not have his explanation of why he left Borchov when he did, or what his plans were. We only have his version as told by his father, Leib Yosef, who had a slanted interest in the telling.

We are reading only one side of the conversation between my grandparents. To be sure, there are passages of Clara's letters that entreat Levi to return to his wife and sons, balanced with others that are sharp and critical in tone. Clara was certainly not a submissive, passive woman. But did she knowingly drive my grandfather out of the house?

Did she live the rest of her life in denial, expecting his eventual return?

Perhaps there is no villain in this story, no guilt to be assigned. Each of the protagonists in this sad tale reacted to events according to his or her ability to appraise a course of action.

And then there was Clara's breakdown. Was it a consequence of my grandfather's departure, leaving her to manage a business that had many debts, along with her need to care for her two young sons, combined with her mother's death? Or was she always high strung?

What did the sanatorium mentioned by cousin Rita provide Clara? Was it the kind of spa that Europeans would visit for rest, rejuvenation and the opportunity to "take the waters," or did it provide her with treatment?

Finally, there was World War I, which prevented any interaction between New York and Borchov and brought much deprivation to the lives of the Borchovers. We do not know what happened during those years that caused Levi to decide not to return to Borchov after the war.

While it is understandable that my uncle would keep the last letters his mother wrote to him, the most puzzling occurrence, to me, is that Levi kept the letters and receipts of money he sent back to Borchov for the rest of his life. What caused him to pack those 1914 letters of explanation and supplication with every move he made?

Did he keep them to show my father and uncle, when they finally joined him in New York, that he'd had good reasons to leave, that he had sent money back for their care, that he'd shown interest and concern for their well-being?

Were these letters the baggage he carried with him all his life? We will never know.

We have been formed by our genes and by our history. Using our knowledge of how we were shaped by those events that occurred a century ago, long before we were born, we live our lives in the present and look to the future with our children and grandchildren.

Let the last words come from my grandmother. In her letter to my grandfather, written over a period of days beginning on 5 May 1914, she wrote:

> There's just one thing that pleases me: if one is lucky from God, He can turn ugliness into beauty and bad into good.

In her letter to her youngest son, Yisroel, whom she called Yisrultzi, written on 22 February 1941, Clara Fahrer Neuringer wrote:

> Now I kiss thousands of times my dear grandchildren. May they be well and grow with much *mazel*. Amen. May God grant that they should not know any misfortune and may you be protected from bad news. Your faithful and good wishing mother who hopes to yet see you in good health and happiness.
>
> Chaiki

Glossary

The words listed here are Hebrew (H), Yiddish (Y), German (G) and Polish (P).

Aktion – G, during WW II, Nazi round-up of Jews for deportation to labor or concentration camps, or mass shootings in the fields and forests beyond the town or city

aleph-bet – H, literally, A, B, the Hebrew alphabet

baal tefillah – H, man who reads from the Torah during services in the synagogue

Bais Ha-Medresh – Y, house of study

bar mitzvah – H, ceremony at age 13, when a boy is considered an adult, ready to fulfill the commandments

belfer – Y, the melamed's assistant, usually in charge of the youngest children

beshert – Y, destiny, "It was meant to be"

bimah – H, elevated platform in the synagogue where the Torah is placed to be read

bór – P, forest

bris – Y, ritual circumcision

brit millah – H, ritual of circumcision.

callah – H, Y, bride

cheder – Y, religious school

cholent – H, a stew made of beans, sometimes with meat, placed in the oven before Shabbos begins on Friday, to cook slowly so that it is ready for the noon meal on Saturday

Chumash – H, book containing the five books of Moses, the Torah

chusen – Y, bridegroom

dos mizinikal – Y, the youngest

Eretz Yisroel – H, Land of Israel

fahrmished – Y, mixed up, in a tizzy

farpitzed – Y, dressed up

gendarme – Y, policeman

get – H, a document of divorce, according to Jewish law

ghetto – perhaps from Italian *getto*, foundry, a set-apart area in a village or city, where Jews were forced to reside goldene medina – Y, the Golden Land, during the years of mass immigration it was the name for America

gymnasium – G, P, Y, high school

hamantashen – H, triangular cakes made for Purim, usually stuffed with prunes or other fruit

hauptman – G, rank in the Austro-Hungarian army, roughly equivalent to captain

kaddish – H, memorial prayer for close relative said during daily services for eleven months

kehilla – H, community

klezmer – Y, traditional Eastern European Jewish music

Kol Nidre – H, the prayer that is said the night before the Day of Atonement begins

knishes – Y, baked, grilled, or deep fried dough with filling, Eastern European snack

kreitzer – Y, (from *Kreuzer*) an Austro-Hungarian coin

kugel – Y, a pudding made of noodles, rice or (during Passover) matzo meal, can be savory or sweet

landsleit – Y, people from the same area

landsman – Y, one who comes from the same community

Landsmanschaften – Y, organizations, often formed by emigrants from the same area to support one another while they got established in their new homes

lockshun – Y, noodles

lulav – H, palm and other tree branches used during Succos celebrations

Magen David – H, the six pointed Star of David

matzo – H, Y, unleavened bread, eaten during the eight days of Passover

mazel – H, good luck, good fortune

mazel tov – H, good luck or congratulations

melamed – Y, teacher of young children in a religious school

mensch – Y, a good-hearted person

meshuggah, meshugganah – Y, crazy, crazy woman

mikvah – H, ritual bath

Mishnah Torah – H, a book of commentary on the Torah (five books of Moses)

mishpocha – Y, extended family

musser – Y, moralizing

naches – Y, joy, pleasure

nishama – Y, soul

oy vay is mir – Y, oh, my goodness!

Parsha Korach, Parsha Shelach – H, the Torah is divided into readings for every week of the year; Parsha refers to a portion; Korach and Shelach refer to particular portions

payes – Y, uncut cut long side curls worn by Orthodox males

Pesach – H, Passover , an eight-day celebration in the spring, commemorating Moses leading the Exodus from Egypt. Unleavened bread called matzo is eaten during these days.

porets – P, nobleman

protectzia – H, favoritism, influence, pull, often secured by a bribe

Purim – H, early spring holiday commemorating the saving of a Jewish population in Persia

pushka – Y, a box where coins for charity was collected

putz – Y, someone acting like a jerk

Rosh Hashanah – H, the beginning of the Jewish New Year in the fall

rov – Y, a title for a learned man

schvitz – Y, steam bath

seder – H, literally "order," the ritual dinner eaten on the first two nights of Passover, during which the Hagaddah (the Passover story) is read

Seudah – H, a small meal eaten late Shabbos afternoon between the afternoon and evening service

Shabbos – Y, the Sabbath, Saturday

Shavous – Y, spring holiday of Shevuot, seven weeks after Pesach, marking the giving of the Torah on Mt. Sinai

shep naches – Y, derive pride and pleasure

shiva – Y, the seven-day period of mourning following the death of a close relative

shloshim – H, literally, thirty; one of the three stages of mourning during the period after a death

shoichet – Y, one who slaughters an animal according to the prescribed ritual, so that the meat will be kosher

shtetl – Y, a small village or town in Eastern Europe

shul – Y, synagogue

simcha – Y, a joyous celebration, such as a bar mitzvah or wedding

Succos – Y, autumn thanksgiving holiday of Sukkot during which people eat their meals in temporary lean-tos

tante – Y, aunt

treif – Y, food that is not kosher

Tsene-rene – Y, condensed version of the Torah, written in Yiddish for women

tzaddik – H, a wise man

tzuris – Y, troubles

yarlmulke – Y, the skullcap worn by men during services in the synagogue and by observant Jews throughout the day

yenta – Y, a woman who gossips, a busybody

yeshivah – Y, a school for religious studies

yizkor – H, literally "remember." The name of the prayer said at the end of certain festivals and on the anniversary of a loved one's death

Yom Alef – H, Sunday

yontif – Y, from "yom tov" (H), "good day," a holiday

Bibliography

Ansky, S. 2003. *The Enemy at His Pleasure: A Journey through the Jewish Pale of Settlement during World War I.* Translated by Joachim Neugroschel. New York: MacMillan.

Beider, Alexander. 2004. *A Dictionary of Jewish Surnames from Galicia.* Bergenfield, NJ: Avotaynu.

Blumenthal, Nachman, ed. 1960. *The Book of Borszczow.* Tel Aviv: I.L. Peretz Publishing.

Kushner, Harold, ed. *Etz Chaim.* 2001 Philadelphia, PA: Rabbinical Assembly, United Synagogue of Conservative Judaism, and Jewish Publication Society.

Megargee, Geoffrey and Dean Martin, eds. 2012. *The Encyclopedia of Camps and Ghettos, 1933 – 1945, Volume II.* Bloomington, IN: Indiana University Press.

Samuel, Maurice. 1943. *The World of Sholom Aleichem.* New York: Knopf Publishing.

Vishniac, Roman. 1999. *Children of a Vanished World.* Mara Vishniac Kohn and Miriam Hartman Flacks, eds. Berkeley, CA: University of California Press.

Acknowledgements

No work of this nature can be written without the assistance, support and encouragement of others. This book would have been stillborn if not for the discoveries made by Adele Neuringer, widow of my Uncle Lee, and Martin Neuringer, my first cousin, and their willingness to entrust me with what they found.

I am, therefore, deeply indebted to Aunt Adele for giving me the memoir my grandfather wrote and to Marty for passing on the packet of letters, postcards and receipts he found in the attic of his father's house in Bethlehem, New Hampshire. We do not know how my uncle came to possess them, but we are thankful he did.

Without Miriam Beckerman's expert translation of all the material, whether written in Yiddish or Hebrew, the stories told by the Yizkor Book, memoir and letters would remain unknown to me and my immediate family. Miriam's knowledge of Jewish history of the period, and her insights into the literature and personalities of the time expanded my understanding of the material. As well, her perseverance in trying to read some of the more illegible passages of the letters must be applauded.

I am indebted to Rachel and Ben Schlesinger for allowing me to borrow many volumes of books from their personal library over the years while I worked on this manuscript. As well, the methods of genealogical research I acquired through my membership in the Jewish Genealogical Society – Toronto and the friendships I made there were a source of inspiration.

Ruth Chernia's editing skills as well as her insistence on historical and stylistic accuracy provided the necessary polish. Greg Ioannou, Kate Unrau, Meghan Behse and the staff at Iguana Press converted the words on the page into a "real book."

Finally, without the understanding, encouragement and skills of my husband, Ed, my first reader, the book would be bereft of the family tree and other visual material.

Ultimately, the interpretation of the memories I have, the material I read, and the conclusions I drew from them are mine.

CPSIA information can be obtained at www.ICGtesting.com
Printed in the USA
LVOW10s1810090616

491939LV00004B/237/P